Arizona State Univ. West Campus Library

CHALK TALKS

FORTY HIGH SCHOOL TEACHERS
SHARE TEACHING TECHNIQUES,
INSIGHTS AND EXPERIENCES . . .
WITH AN APPENDIX OF COMMENTS
BY SENIOR STUDENTS (Class of '85)

CHALK TALKS

A Practical Operational Perspective of Real Teaching

A15040 169990

Edited by

CATHERINE E. SCHWARZ

Howell High School
Howell, Michigan

LB
1607
.C42
1987
West

Arizona State Univ. West Campus Library

CHARLES C THOMAS • PUBLISHER
Springfield • Illinois • U. S. A.

Published and Distributed Throughout the World by

CHARLES C THOMAS • PUBLISHER
2600 South First Street
Springfield, Illinois 62794-9265

This book is protected by copyright. No part of
it may be reproduced in any manner without
written permission from the publisher.

© *1987 by* CHARLES C THOMAS • PUBLISHER
ISBN 0-398-05350-2
Library of Congress Catalog Card Number: 87-6513

With THOMAS BOOKS *careful attention is given to all details of manufacturing and design. It is the Publisher's desire to present books that are satisfactory as to their physical qualities and artistic possibilities and appropriate for their particular use.* THOMAS BOOKS *will be true to those laws of quality that assure a good name and good will.*

Printed in the United States of America
Q-R-3

Library of Congress Cataloging in Publication Data
Chalk talks.

1. High school teaching. 2. High school teaching--
United States. I. Schwarz, Catherine E.
LB1607.C42 1987   373.11'02   87-6513
ISBN 0-398-05350-2

FOREWORD

THIRTY-SEVEN years ago I began collecting tips gathered out of my experience in supervising graduate students teaching the Introductory Psychology course. As the compendium of tips grew, I mimeographed them and distributed them to the teaching fellows in order that they might use them to avoid some of the problems encountered by beginning teachers.

As the graduate students spread around the country teaching psychology at various colleges and universities, they wrote back for copies of the "teaching tips" and eventually the load became great enough that I decided to put the tips into book form. The result was the book *Teaching Tips,* now in its eighth edition (D. C. Heath, 1986).

I'm pleased to see that Catherine Schwarz has developed a similar enterprise for classroom teachers in high school. I've enjoyed reading *Chalk Talks,* and I think many other teachers will also enjoy and profit from it. Beginning teachers will find a wealth of practical teaching techniques to fortify them against possible discouragement in a difficult first year.

It is true that much in teaching depends upon the accumulated wisdom of experienced teachers and that we all have much to gain by sharing our experiences, insights, and our techniques. *Chalk Talks* will, I'm sure, provide a useful medium for extending the dialogue between teachers.

Wilbert J. McKeachie

Editor's Note: University of Michigan psychologist Professor Wilbert J. McKeachie is a research scholar at the University Center for Research on Learning and Teaching.

PREFACE

CHALK TALKS is a collection of candid, spontaneous statements of Howell High School teachers and administrators, initially intended for the H.H.S. Professional Staff. Forty experienced teachers share a variety of proven teaching practices, here organized into seven short chapters. Footnote numbers identify contributors, as acknowledgement and also for further contact and discussion.

An Appendix presents related statements of students just before their graduation from Howell High (June, 1985). They comment on their teachers — candidly.

The entire faculty was invited and encouraged to participate in this voluntary project. The forty who eventually contributed did so at the expense of personal free time. Perhaps some responses were hurried; others were written with considerable care.

I am grateful to my professional colleagues who, in these pages, share some of their methods, helpful suggestions, and insights. I am impressed anew with the competence and goodness of the professionals dedicated to the education of Howell High School students.

Contributors to *Chalk Talks* represent the following departments: Administration; Business; Counseling and Guidance; Data Processing, English; Foreign Language; Health Occupations; Home Economics; Library and Media; Mathematics, Science, Social Studies; Special Education; Technical and Industrial; and Vocational Education.

* * * * *

During the 1985-1986 school year, while teaching a full schedule within the English Department, I spent many weekends and some vacation and holiday time to bring this project to completion. My husband, John—himself a master teacher at high school, university, and adult education levels—was my primary advisor. I also thank Dr. Wilbert J. McKeachie, Director, Center for Research on Learning and Teaching, University of Michigan; Dr. Alan H. Jones, Publisher and Executive Editor, *The Education Digest;* Dr. Jack W. Meiland, Associate Dean, College of Literature, Science and the Arts, University of Michigan; and Dr. Raymond E. Gatza, Education Administrator. Each assisted me with valuable service.

Richard Bologna, Howell High School Principal, supported the endeavor from the start. Here I record my thanks to him and to all who so generously helped.

The first typed draft revealed diversity of style, much repetition, and over-lapping. In editing the work I sought some minimal uniformity of style and reduction of repetition. This I assumed as an editor's privilege and responsibility.

Originally considered for limited and local professional development, the general audience of *Chalk Talks* has expanded. *Chalk Talks* is appropriate for professional teachers everywhere. Staff Development Administrators will welcome it. Principals and teachers in many schools can use it to spark similar sharing. Teachers, grades 5-12, will discover in *Chalk Talks* proven methods to use. College professors will find it a valuable supplement to texts in education courses.

If *Chalk Talks* helps to promote productive discussion, and if the sharing of ideas helps in any way to improve the already excellent education available to our high school students, and students in other schools as well, the project is a worthwhile and honorable expenditure of time and effort.

Catherine E. Schwarz

INTRODUCTION

Education is a continual, and difficult work to be done by kindness, by watching, by warning, by precept, and by praise, but above all — by example.

— John Ruskin, English Essayist

HIGH SCHOOL is a major part of education. For some it is the foundation for college; for others, employment or United States Service; for most, life itself.

Most adults recall vividly their high school years — classmates, some favorite teacher(s), activities, events, episodes. High school years span that unique period of "growing up." It is less personalized than elementary grades, yet more so than college. For most students it is a period of intense socialization (peer pressure), shared experiences (classes, teachers, schedules, activities), of issues of security and sense of belonging (sought, achieved — or both).

High school teachers have a challenging — sometimes enjoyable, sometimes difficult — responsibility: primarily to teach high school youth the designated subject matter within an approved curriculum.

Most high school students are cooperative, especially if the class is of interest to them. Most look forward to more social aspects of school — class exchange, lunch time — and to the freedom of dismissal, week-ends, vacations. They do what is necessary to pass from grade to grade and eventually graduate.

Some students are highly motivated, industrious, self-controlled, interested in and desirous of learning. Others are insecure, distracted, or apathetic, unable or unwilling to put forth the necessary effort without teacher intervention. Some may be self-centered, rebellious, even disruptive at times.

These are some reasons *Chalk Talks* treats not only teaching but also motivation, classroom management, rapport, discipline, organization, and miscellaneous "bits of this and that."

A WORD ABOUT THE FORMAT IN THIS BOOK:

The various contributors are identified by the number in parenthesis after each statement. These contributors and their academic areas are listed on page 99. Throughout the book each new statement is indicated visually by •.

PRINCIPAL'S NOTE

IT IS IMPORTANT to me that educators take time from their work and personal lives to think about the youth they have taught and the techniques they have used. It is even more important that they write them down to share, as the contributors to *Chalk Talks* have done.

Howell High School has a long, rich tradition. The first graduation recorded was in 1869. Today our new high school complex houses 1850 students, 100 teachers and support staff. Over 63 percent of the professional staff hold a Master's degree at least, and have a minimum of ten years teaching experience. Howell High School offers a complete academic curriculum with a strong vocational component.

Our community is changing and diversified. Primarily a country region, Howell has a few residents whose families have been here for generations. Some families have moved to the area in the past fifteen years, while continuing to work in the surrounding cities—Lansing, Detroit, Ann Arbor.

It has been and continues to be our challenge to offer our students an education which is academically sound and comprehensive, in an atmosphere which meets the expectations of our changing community.

We are trying to maintain an environment in which the self-respect, creativity, and safety of each individual is encouraged and has a chance to grow. We are convinced that this depends, to a large degree, on open communication, mutual respect, and cooperation of all members of the Howell Public Schools' community.

Richard Bologna, Principal

CONTENTS

CHALK TALKS

- *A teacher affects eternity; he can never tell where his influence stops.*

  -Henry Adams,
  The Education of Henry Adams

- *In the opinion of fools teaching is a humble task, but in fact it is the noblest of occupations.*

  -Erasmus

1

- *Rule .1: The teacher is never wrong. Rule .2: If the teacher is wrong, refer to Rule .1.*

  -Seen on a T-shirt in New Guinea

CHAPTER 1

ON TEACHING

"GOOD TEACHERS have made a lasting impression on my life. These teachers encouraged me to do my best and never gave up," wrote a Howell High School senior before his recent graduation.

Most writing about teaching and education is theoretical; most comes from university Ph.D.s, associates in schools of education, researchers. Research on teaching and learning goes its own abstract way, while real teachers here and now try concretely to improve techniques, classroom environment, conditions under which their students learn.

Chalk Talks is practical, written by experienced high school teachers. This is the educational "real world" — and these are techniques in use that "work."

Appropriately, *Chalk Talks* begins with the chapter "On Teaching."

* * * * *

A. Best Ideas Come From . . .

- Teachers who have taught the class earlier, and from my own digging through resources in the library. (11)
- I think of some ideas to experiment with. Ideas come from students; ideas come from other teachers also. The main thing is to try the new ideas out. If they bomb (students will tell you) throw them out but modify and/or keep the good ones. (8)

- Teachers in my field (Language) sharing ideas. It might be a good idea to have staff share at department meetings. Those teaching the same subject or course can use the ideas readily (i.e. using wordless cartoons or photos from papers or ads for conversation, or ideas from education games). Foreign language journals have interesting articles with ideas to vary methods in class. I think sharing with colleagues is **invaluable.** (6)
- Other teachers, conventions, journals, films, and filmstrips, tapes, books, experience. (13)
- Magazines: *Media and Methods;* also *The Book Report.* For professional reading, you can't beat *Phi Delta Kappan.* These and other periodicals are available in the Howell High School Library. (32)
- Remembering and practicing excellent teaching methods of those who taught me — my parents, grade and high school teachers, university professors, thousands of students I have taught and from whom I have learned, fellow teachers, and others. (35)
- Reading professional literature regularly, especially *English Journal.* Talking with other teachers about their methods. Reading *New York Times, Atlantic,* and other periodicals regularly, and using selected articles. Regional Educational Media Center (R.E.M.C.) is useful for films on various subjects. (15)
- Classes taken at Michigan State University and Lansing Community College, exchanging ideas with other teachers, television, viewing plays. (33)
- Discussion with other teachers, students, my own children. Most of my ideas come from my own imagination or a specific Teacher's Manual. I use variation on a theme. Exploring the library on my own, and asking for help from the Media Specialists. I would like an AV list correlated to textbook material I use. I try to do some of this in the library. (31)
- Reading publications such as the *Journal of Reading, English Teacher,* NCTE *Notes Plus,* and by discussing and sharing different ideas with fellow language arts teachers. Yearly I attend several conferences which provide new ideas and approaches to teaching language arts skills. At times I purchase professional books which suggest good ideas and materials. (17)

- Professional workshops and publications for classroom use are my major resources. I attend the Michigan Council of Teachers of Mathematics Convention each year. M.C.T.M. publishes helpful booklets of ideas, examples, and techniques for classroom use. (38)
- Remembering how boring, although calming, routine can be. I haven't been at this high school long enough to feel I have the one best method or to know who can suggest a better one, or where to look. (18)
- Talking with other mathematics teachers during lunch has been the most effective source of ideas for me. I get many ideas from my professional peers. (24)
- Selected local and national newspapers as well as magazine articles, books, movies, television specials, plays, travel, sports . . . life itself. I observe students closely, try to be sensitive to them, consult with them, respect their opinions and suggestions. Fellow teachers are rich and generous sources of ideas. Frequent discussions with my husband, John—himself an experienced master teacher—produce a variety of interesting, helpful ideas and suggestions. I use libraries frequently—our high school, Ann Arbor Public, University of Michigan, and the Educational Resource Information Center (E.R.I.C.) at the University of Michigan. Professors are occasional consultants and resource persons also. (35)
- Professional journals, e.g. *American Vocational Journal,* and *School Shop.* Also Technical-Industrial conferences; participating in North Central Accreditation evaluations; meeting with other teachers; reference files, and work experience. (34)
- Workshops, co-ed magazines, textbooks, and other teachers, and TV specials which relate to my teaching area (Home Economics). I've shown the video-tape "Shattered Spirits," discussed co-dependency with students, and then invited the Health Occupations teacher to come to discuss her workshop on co-dependency with my class. (37)

B. *Implementing Good Ideas and Practices . . .*

- I always tell students what to look for before showing any film or video tape. I ask for a written summary after the film is shown, or have prepared questions for discussion. (36)

- In practical psychology, students seem to get involved in activities that mostly deal with interpersonal relationships, in which they can compare their concept of some aspect of themselves with others who'll give feedback. Also, I use a few movies demonstrating interpersonal relations, for example, *The Big Chill* and final "M.A.S.H." TV episodes. (3)
- Many practical helps for teaching writing come from attending conferences. In 1986 I attended my first N.C.T.E. Conference. I will never miss one again. I returned from San Antonio, Texas, feeling recharged, ready to conquer the world of teen-age intellectual learning and writing problems. Outstanding ideas were presented at the Conference from teachers and book company representatives from across the country. I was treated as the professional I am. I can't emphasize strongly enough the importance of the N.C.T.E. annual conference for all teachers of English. (30)
- For low achievers in language arts, I keep alert to TV programs which correlate with textbook assignments. I use newspaper items, travel brochures, ads (K-Mart, Kroger, etc.) and menus to plan lessons for low achievers. I make spelling lists related to holidays, seasons, clothing, foods, the state of Michigan, national events, etc. . . . (4)
- In making assignments I try to think how the material can be interestingly related to personal interests of the students. I try to imagine myself writing the assignment, and ask myself, "Would I enjoy it?" "What could I learn from it?" (15)
- I use a dittoed outline or hand-out of the day's topics to which students can add their notes as we talk. Students find these notes easy to study later. I can see if class members are taking notes. I call on them if they are not. (16)
- Allowing more than one choice of essay topic helps both teacher and students. Having three or four approved essay topics allows selection by the student, and increases the chances of getting the students' interest. The selection helps the teacher break the monotony of grading a large stack of papers all on the same subject. (9)
- A large part of my teaching centers on positive reinforcement of some standard rules of writing well (once the student is mas-

tering spelling, vocabulary, reading, and writing skills). Films, plays, poems, and literature in general can be useful. (10)

- I use the handbook *College Thinking: How to Get the Best Out of College* by Jack W. Meiland with senior-level advanced English students. It challenges college-bound seniors **to think,** explains differences between high school and college, and helps students acquire a basic understanding of the methods and purposes of college work. (Mentor Books. New American Library, 1981). (35)
- In teaching the German language, whenever possible I try to conjure up a crazy name for a new concept, something that will help students remember what it is. "Shoe verbs" (a line around non-changing forms looks like a shoe), "machine-gun verbs" (past tense forms sound like rat-a-tat-tat) and "purple mushrooms" (German subjunctive, because it's so unreal!) are a few samples. My best ideas spring from a desire to make something as understandable as possible for students. I see it as my great goal in life to simplify German, to codify it, to present it all neatly tied up in separate little packages. Ideas for assignments come from asking myself what a situation might demand of a student. Some days, I pretend I can't understand English at all, and students try everything they can think of to communicate with me. Sometimes, I'll lapse into English with a heavy German or Russian accent so students can get used to hearing how a foreign-born person speaks our language. I've used ideas from *Games* magazine, from *Omni,* and others. I encourage students to apply their foreign language abilities to computer projects. (27)
- I find many high school students are not accustomed to working in small groups, brain-storming, putting examples on the board, nor using opaque and over-head projectors. Therefore, I teach students to develop these skills. (18)
- I try to remember that the purpose of education is to teach students to think. Therefore, I never show filmstrips, nor do I try to just lecture. Rather, I attempt to use the Socratic Method, i.e., I ask the students questions designed to make them think. I call on students even if they don't raise their hands. When I need a rest I show movies about history, not Hollywood productions. (19)

- A technique I find effective in teaching a foreign language in the classroom is personally to involve the students while activating the specific language. Learning a foreign language can easily seem abstract and irrelevant to the students unless they have opportunities to express something about themselves. Even at the first year level, I give students the necessary tools to say something. It may be "I like to play football" or "I don't like to cook." They answer in the foreign language. In a chapter dealing with family members, rather than having students simply memorize a list of words like father, uncle, or sister, I have them give short oral presentations describing their family trees. In an upper level class, I spend a portion of the class session on Monday asking students what they did over the weekend, giving them the opportunity to express their experiences in a foreign language. I find that this integration of real experiences in the foreign language helps students internalize the vocabulary and integrate language skills more effectively. (23)

- Whenever possible, I use the questioning method to help improve students' thought power. I ask, wait, encourage, then accept and appreciate reflective answers or thoughtful questions. I encourage students to express their views. I try always to exemplify and teach tolerance and respect for self, for others, for students, and for their differing views. (35)

- In English classes, my students regularly take part in reading plays. Students volunteer to read and act out (on a limited basis) a particular character's role. Some students clear the front of the classroom which becomes the stage. A narrator volunteers; props and sound effects are simple. The student-actors move about "on stage" and make appropriate gestures. They change facial expressions and vocal tones, responsive to the text. Teacher and students who have neither a reading nor acting role participate as the attentive, respectful audience. (Grades 9 and 10 performed *The Miracle Worker, Antigone, Our Town, Medea, Twelve Angry Men, Romeo and Juliet, Julius Caesar* and other plays in this manner during a single school year.) (35)

- To help students understand Shakespeare's classic drama *Julius Caesar,* I first teach students the ancient history of Julius Caesar and the geography of his world and times (basis of the Shakespearean work). I use maps and materials purchased at Stratford, Ontario. I help students learn names and personalities of Shakespeare's major and minor characters, and, as necessary, give them the story line, or paraphrase a difficult passage. Students memorize some famous quotations. The H.H.S. Media Center's VCR *Julius Caesar* is very helpful as a teaching resource. Other English teachers use the same or similar methods. (35)

- Recently some sophomore students reading a short story set in the Depression era asked, "What caused the Great Depression?" I spent lunch-time that noon in the Social Studies Office where knowledgeable teachers discussed the matter. Steve Manor, a U.S. history teacher, loaned me a book which enabled me to give an accurate, brief outline of causes to classes reading the story. Because students had asked the question, they were motivated to pay attention to the historical account of factors influencing the Great Depression. This helped them understand their own reading assignment better and prepared them for further learning; it demonstrated interrelatedness of academic disciplines, and also faculty team-work. (35)

- To teach the history of computers, I use the filmstrip series *From Pebbles to Computers*. To cover an idea in teaching a computer concept, I use a worksheet that exemplifies that concept. I use the help of community resource people to back up and strengthen a concept taught; such as personal finance, insurance, and legal rights of consumers. (7) (Editor's Note: *From Pebbles to Computers* Filmstrip available in high school Media Center.)

- Study, the processes by which we learn, requires self-discipline. Study is, above all, hard work. Learning to study well makes the effort easier. The student who has learned to study is prepared in the best sense for work in college, and for life in the real world. Whatever helps the student to learn to study is, therefore, an important contribution to his education. The three basic study skills are: (1.) the skill of finding what you want; (2.) the skill of fixing it in your mind; and (3.) the skill of organizing it for use.

Dr. Francis P. Robinson (in *Effective Study*, Harper and Brothers, 1946) reduced the method of acquiring the three study skills to a formula: Q3R. The Q represents question. If we turn an assignment into the question "What am I supposed to learn?" we become aware of what we want to find. This same question can be asked for each paragraph or unit of the assignment.

3R represents read, recite, review. We read to answer the question or questions. We close the book, recite the answer, and do so for all parts of the assignment. When we have finished the entire assignment we review with the purpose of organizing the material for future use. (From *Study Is Hard Work*, William Armstrong. Harper and Row. Lippincott Publishers, Inc.) (35)

- Recently I took an excellent course in teaching reading at the secondary level. This course can be especially helpful when the textbook work is combined with a program of practical application. I'd recommend such a course for all high school teachers. (Curriculum 636 at Eastern Michigan University, 1985-86 — currently required in all educational programs at master degree level.) (40)

- Some of my best ideas have come from observation of the business community. Also, advisory committees of local business people have been helpful. They have provided me with extra materials and leads on good films. One local business person put together an entire unit for me a few years ago. (21)

- Teaching Health Occupations is very different from teaching an academic course. When I began teaching about twelve years ago there were limited textbooks for Nursing Assistant skills. Now I use *Diversified Health Occupations* with my classes. This textbook reflects the diversification of the field of health care, and provides students with a much broader perspective. (14)

- My teacher training was in Competency-Based Educational Methods, and I work from clear State Performance Objectives. I usually attend two field-related conferences each year, provided by Michigan State University in cooperation with the Department of Education. I'm very involved with both the professional organization "Michigan Health Occupations Educators" (MHOE) and the student organization "Health Occupations Students of America" (HOSA). As President Elect of MHOE for 1985-1986, I sit on the advisory board for State HOSA. (14)

- I regularly attend workshops and professional organization meetings, and I "network" with other local and state home economics teachers. (40)
- During summers I work in machine shops. I find "real world" machining practices have more value in my teaching than practices I learned in college. (28)
- My areas, mechanical drawing and graphics, are fairly straightforward. I try to maintain current knowledge through reading numerous magazines and newspapers. Occasionally I photograph new homes under construction for my own information and to present students with pictures of actual building practices and details. (29)
- I try to help students develop and improve thinking and communication skills, poise, self-confidence, leadership, and mutual respect . . . as well as knowledge. To help achieve these, twice each month each class participates in a discussion. An appropriate topic is democratically decided by each class beforehand, then prepared by reading, thought, and sometimes research. As experience is gained, different students in each class take over the role of discussion leader.

  I teach ninth graders and other students to use the *Reader's Guide to Periodical Literature,* to research various topics, to outline and take notes, to study, and to prepare for a speech or to take part in class discussion. (35)
- First, the school is a human community. As such, we teach students the subject matter. Master teachers place students first, and adapt their teaching of subject matter to the needs of each particular class.

  Second, the effective classroom teacher draws on a large bag of tricks. Creativity is not essential, but being a creative thief of ideas is of value.

  Third, viewing the class as a live audience is helpful. We must remember that a passive audience learns little. Learning is an active experience. (26)

QUESTIONS FOR DISCUSSION

Many questions pertain to statements in the text. The first several words of each such statement are given, with precise location for easy reference.

1. Teaching has been called "an art," "a science," "a challenge and privilege," "a subversive activity," "stressful employment," "over-paid baby-sitting" . . . With which expression(s) do you agree? Why?
2. How do **you** define education? teaching? learning? Is teaching possible without learning?
3. Do you agree with the quotation from John Ruskin? (cf. Introduction, p. ix) Discuss.
4. Henry Adams wrote, "A teacher affects eternity." How is this true? How can this truth enter the daily classroom?
5. How can teachers in this school share teaching techniques so all can benefit? What teaching technique(s) are you willing to share?
6. How can this teaching staff (team) benefit from workshops, conferences, and graduate classes which some members attend? How can we learn from one another by sharing these experiences?
7. Do you believe some or most teaching methods which are effective in such subjects as mathematics, science, business, or shop can be effective also in English, Social Studies, Foreign Languages, and other subjects? Are teaching skills transferable? Give examples.
8. Is shared responsibility possible between counselors and classroom teachers? Between the principal, assistant principals, and teachers? Can one ease the burden and increase the effectiveness of the other? Is shared responsibility possible?
9. Is team work and spirit possible among professionals on this staff. How can we improve?
10. (a.) What can teachers do to promote and strengthen team spirit in each department?, among professionals in this school? (b.) How could more interaction and professional discussion among teachers here improve the educational opportunity and accomplishments of students in this school?

• *Motivation grows out of interest.*
If one can see the reason for
doing some task which is
assigned, the task becomes easier.

-William Armstrong,
Study Is Hard Work

2

• *Report from a classroom,*
overheard in a discussion: "Well,
a girl knows when she falls in
love with a boy but a boy doesn't
even know that the girl's in love
with him or whatever, and
doesn't know much of anything —
so girls are more mature."

CHAPTER 2

ON MOTIVATION

ALTHOUGH good teaching takes many forms, important re-sources for its success reside within the students themselves when they enter the classroom. As a good athletic coach needs capable, motivated players to succeed, so too good teachers do best with capable, motivated students. Teaching efforts are challenged, often hampered by unmotivated, unwilling, distracted or reluctant students.

Factors including maturity, talents, aptitudes, and abilities of students as well as their interests, motives, attitudes, and values, influence the teacher's instructional impact. Students will usually perceive the teacher's special effort as showing that he/she cares and is striving to offer a worthwhile course.

Professional high school teachers here share some of their methods and special efforts.

* * * * *

- On a weekly basis, I try to inform classes where we are heading in our study of German so that there is the feeling that a light at the end of the tunnel really does exist. If a student is having difficulty with the subject, I try to relate it in terms of his/her hobbies or where his/her interests lie. "Well, you know, German is a lot like playing with model trains. . . . " That way, German can be thought of in terms of analogies rather than dry grammar and obscure rules. I do use the same terminology correctly over and over so that eventually a student can talk to me in the "jargon" I've been using in class: "prepositions in the dative case," "past tense of strong verbs," etc. (27)

- Other than the usual appeals to logic and building the future they will someday have, I try to make students realize I always expect them to try their best. (3)

- I explain policy and goals for the year/lesson/assignment to help students understand and fulfill my expectations. Students have more incentive when they understand how compliance with requirements now will benefit them in college, in life. I work with students to help them attain goals. I make sure they know the process which leads to success. Assigning them to read the chapter and answer questions does not prepare them well for a test *unless* they have been taught how to find, study, and learn important information. We must ask questions in class which challenge higher thinking skills and show students how to answer thoughtfully. Only then can we expect them to answer such questions on tests. (6)

- I offer suggestions and encouragement, but don't lower expectations. I try to know the ability of each individual in class for this, but it doesn't always work. I have been fairly successful though. "Use your best judgment" is a phrase I have been kidded about. One class bought me a shirt with this printed on it. Some test or bonus questions also encourage thinking. (8)

- First I use goals and competition to motivate; next, I use pride and responsibility as support. Then I give students my philosophy about why they should work hard to learn:

  they become more interesting;
  they learn to think;
  they learn responsibility;
  they learn pride;
  they find jobs. (19)

- I have found when a class has a large number of students not doing homework it helps to pick up their homework directly from them. When students do not have their homework, I can speak directly to each about that problem. The result is an increased percentage of students completing their homework, and doing it more often. This process gives me an opportunity to establish personal contact with students more frequently than I would normally. This is helpful in establishing better rapport. (20)

- A poster in my classroom states: "IF YOU THINK SCHOOL IS BORING, WAIT UNTIL YOU'RE IN THE UNEMPLOYMENT LINE." (3)
- Give encouragement, compliment work well done (a smile, a word, a pat on the back). Be positive about what you expect, and positively expect the student to do that work. (4)
- Set high goals. Explain clearly, then expect students to achieve these goals. (37)
- I have seen simulation games used to develop skills we all dream of using to help students achieve. Any time spent in sharing, discussing, and preparing such simulations is well spent. By simulation games is meant role-play situations simulating real life, for example: World Affairs—Balance of Power; World Water Shortage, Competition for Natural Resources; World Hunger. Also National Affairs—Our Legal System, Unemployment, etc. The purpose is to teach content, competition, cooperation, decision-making skills.

  A class is divided into groups of five or six. Each is given a goal and a role to play. The teacher set-up is quite extensive; student participation is generally excellent. Games go on for a week or so of class time. (32)
- Be well prepared. Get the students' mental attention. Explain the value of the lesson; relate it to what they already know whenever possible. Then, as has been said, "Tell them what you are going to tell them. Then tell them. Next tell them what you told them. Then ask them to tell you what you told them. Then tell them where they're wrong (or right)!" (35)
- I strive to explain the logic of each unit of study and include both scope and sequences, i.e. some units are difficult but necessary to provide a proper foundation for future studies. (39)
- Work consistently and correctly completed can be rewarded; e.g. a student may receive a desired library permit for reading, research, or study for one class hour. (4)

- Grading is done in the presence of each student. I commend progress and respond to questions the student may have. (25)
- Discuss the realities of the job market. Ask students what they hope to do with their future; point out how the class will help them achieve their goal(s). Set due dates for a series of assignments — so students learn to budget time. (5)
- As teacher of the business class/enterprise "KORNER STORE," I give the students responsible jobs to be done. I encourage them to try even if not sure of themselves. It's important to be very understanding if mistakes are made. It's important, also, that students see the consequence of their decision, whether good or bad. Students need to be encouraged to **learn** from mistakes; then mistakes become learning experiences. (21)
- Challenge students to think. For example, teach them to accept the Poetry Unit. Ugh! Begin with familiar nursery rhymes, or Dr. Seuss. Help them enjoy the rhyme and rhythm. The Media Center has two excellent filmstrips on how to teach poetry. Frequently change pace. Grade assigned writing for thought and self-expression with one mark; grade spelling and mechanics of writing separately, when students know what is expected. Careful corrections on written assignments become individualized teaching, tutoring. (31)
- While motivating and helping students, I think one of the most important things to keep in mind is that they are unique individuals with equally unique motivations. Take each case as it comes. Find out **who** that person is and **where** he/she is before trying to help a student get where you want him/her to go. (23)
- I like to assign individual work stressing that its completion is a sign of personal responsibility, growth, and maturity. Use students as cross-peer tutors. (2)
- Make sure the work is within students' instructional level, that they understand the task, and that success is possible for every class member. (12)
- Use sequence of "What-if?" or "What next?" questions after each discussion to foster continued thoughts and decisions. Have students role-play real life situations to see results which occur when consequences are not thought out beforehand. (2)

- Use open-ended sentences, and paradoxes. Ask students to analyze a situation someone else may be in; evaluate various courses of action as well as possible consequences for each. (3)
- I detail the objectives of the class at the beginning of the term. I tell students what they should learn, and what I expect in terms of achievement and behavior. I use a grading system that permits all students to get an "A" if they do the required work well, correcting it as I indicate. Students know their grade each week and decide if they want to get that grade, or relax their efforts and get a lower grade. Very few choose the latter. However, this places the burden of performance in their hands. **In my regular classes** I tell students that they don't have "free" days. I am here to teach; they are here to learn. I adjust the difficulty of class assignments, and build in "fun" (activities) on days before holidays and the like. However, there is a lesson to be learned even on those occasions. **In the reading lab** with basic students, however, I do allow students to play computer games every second Friday if all their work is completed. If it isn't, it is "make-up day." (17)
- I have a chart in the classroom listing weekly requirements. When students complete them, I check them off or write in the score received. I call on all students during class discussions, and wait for those who need time to think out and phrase their answer. I sometimes use structured overviews to introduce a difficult lesson and the ideas and terms to be considered. I have students keep notebooks and folders with their work. There are many built-in motivators in the reading lab that keep students working and trying, the least of which is completing computer-assisted instruction on the micros. I vary the materials students use to match their abilities. Students know I will help them as well as I can, also that I expect their sincere effort in return. (17)
- Students often produce what is expected, but we need to be reasonable. Let every student experience some success. I develop questions and activities to help students develop critical thinking skills. (13)
- I assign group work where others depend on the individual student. Also I re-write sessions with individual help before, during and after drama class. (33)

- I keep students' written work throughout the year in a folder, to be reviewed periodically in a student-teacher conference. The conference focuses on assessment of individual progress, goals, and strategies to achieve goals. (15)
- I compliment good thought process, and encourage acceptance of any idea as effort. I go around and discuss individually with each student those assignments which are missing—causing a lower grade. I give extra credit for "early" essays or speeches. This often "turns on" a reluctant member who is afraid he/she is less capable. This way **effort** gets a compliment and a grade boost for the student. (18)
- All of my students keep a record of completed assignments and of the grade earned. This keeps them informed of achievement and aware of their progress. (22)
- I set short-term and long-term goals. I give special credit for work some students complete at home and in the community. Students receive literary credit for reading, and for individual or group assignments in writing. Students write letters of application and of recommendation for practical experience. (10)
- I find this to be the most difficult area of teaching. I do not feel I have found anything that works as motivation. I believe all I can do is keep expecting their best and accepting no less. I will not lower my standards set for them and I hope they will rise to meet them eventually. It may take weeks and several progress reports before students realize that half a job isn't going to 'do it' for them. Finally, many decide to produce. I make it clear I am available after school each day to help. Also, I insist all make-up tests are taken after school so that they will not miss another class just because they have missed the original test. (11)
- Giving many small tests rather than just a few big ones seems to motivate students to study on a day-to-day basis. Making comments on student papers when they do well is also encouraging and motivates them to continue to do well. (7)
- Each semester I begin by assisting students to set some academic and personal goals, even short-term objectives. I often give students the opportunity to evaluate their own work as well as the work of others. I encourage constructive feedback. In the class-

room I display posters, newspaper articles on current issues, and informational handouts. I change these regularly to encourage students to notice and read them. This helps make the learning environment more interesting, and is one way to get students to read. When helping students I lean over, may lightly touch them as I speak (if that is comfortable) and reinforce their efforts. (40)

- Individual contracts are effective. Also I require students to give their line of thought and reasoning when they answer some questions. At times I photograph students' projects for later display in Talent-a-Rama, the display case, yearbook, or newspaper. I take pictures of students at work, also. (34) (Editor's Note: Talent-a-Rama: annual organized display of selected K-12 student projects and accomplishments in academic, vocational, creative and performing arts areas. For public awareness and appreciation.)

- At the beginning of a semester I sometimes have students fill out a questionnaire on goals. This gives the opportunity to think about a future occupation, college attendance, or military service. Also, some questions apply to the current course of study — their interest, motivation, and intentions to work for a good grade. With mathematics classes it works well to graph pre-tests in one color and the finished progress test in another. Students then see readily if they are achieving their goal. (38)

- Students are motivated, at least in part, when the teacher expresses excitement about the subject. I let them see I like the subject and enjoy it. Beyond "teaching the book" - when the teacher is interested or even excited for some reason, students catch hold and will try. It's good to make students laugh, to ask them questions, to play the "Devil's Advocate" at times. (30)

- The clinical experience which is part of the Health Occupations course is very important for the individual student in terms of motivation and clarifying goals. The classroom learning process relates application of information and experiences to individual goals and values. (14)

- Obviously outlines of class expectations are necessary, but motivation is best encouraged when students see fellow classmates working and achieving. Once in a while progress reports or a discussion with mom/dad/gram/gramps, etc., are necessary. Usually analyzing a problem step-by-step helps an unsure student develop powers of thinking, analyzing, and evaluating. (29)

- I allow students the opportunity to do an assignment a second time. They may also retake tests after school to help them improve their knowledge and grade. (37)

- I do not believe that in the purest sense we can motivate students. Rather, our job is to create the conditions for self-motivation. This is best done by establishing clear goals and objectives, both short and long range; providing a variety of experiences (e.g. small and large group work as well as individual); creating a comfortable setting; making our subject relevant to ourselves and our students. (26)

- The teacher's presentation is best received, understood, and retained when students are capable, interested, attentive, and motivated to achieve. Student interest is strengthened when the material is demonstrably related (a.) to other knowledge already possessed by students, (b.) to purposes and goals of the students and of the course work, (c.) to the overall curriculum goals, (d.) when possible, to future educational and/or employment plans of students. (35)

- Students who understand that education is their wisest investment establish educational goals and priorities, build internal productivity habits, and actively participate in their own education. (26)

■

QUESTIONS FOR DISCUSSION

1. Given varying degrees of student interest, maturity, ability, etc., how can teachers make some success possible for every student, even the least capable?

2. Motivation comes from within and is related to student self interest. Since interest is fundamental to every kind of study, how can teachers help students acquire and develop an interest in learning? in learning particular subjects?

3. Teachers can "turn students off," close rather than open their minds. How? How can teachers inspire students to want to learn?

4. Some high school seniors are quoted in *Chalk Talks*. They comment on teacher strengths: "Qualities Students Consider Desirable in Teachers" (cf. Appendix pp. 93-94). How can these observations be helpful?

5. The students also identify and comment on teacher limitations: "Qualities of Poor Teachers" (cf. Appendix pp. 95-97). Are these criticisms valid? constructive? useful? How?

6. Exterior as well as interior motivations influence adults. Consider, for example: reward, recognition, constructive criticism. Exterior motivations also influence students. What exterior motivations help inspire students to learn? to be open-minded? to seek knowledge on their own? Give specific examples.

7. "First I use goals and competition to motivate . . ." (19) p. 18. Is this a technique you use or could use in your classroom? How?

8. Relating content you teach to the "real world" — life after graduation, the job market — can help motivate students. How do you do this? Share.

9. Consider the poster statement: "If you think high school is boring, wait until you're in the unemployment line." (3) p. 19. How could this and similar maxims help motivate students? Do you know of others to share?

10. "Fear will not motivate to goodness, but . . . " (26), p. 33. (a.) Is this statement idealistic? realistic? true? (b.) How can teachers practice this principle in the classroom?

● *Teachers who believe they are in control of what goes on within their classrooms tend to be more effective than those who feel powerless, overworked or insecure.*

-Duke and Meckel, Teacher's Guide to Classroom Management

3

● *Report from a classroom, a test in health studies: "To prevent head colds, use an agonizer to spray nose until it drops into your throat."*

● *Report from a classroom, a history test: "The French Revolution was caused by overcharging taxies."*

CHAPTER 3

ON CLASSROOM MANAGEMENT

MANAGING the classroom effectively is essential to good teaching. Classroom management includes first creating and then maintaining an environment in which both teaching and learning can occur. There is no single best method. No single set of practices works well in every circumstance, nor for everyone.

Although general principles apply, classroom management methods and style are best decided by individual teachers. One's method is much influenced by personality, motivations, interests, attitudes, educational background and preparedness, teaching experience, talents and abilities.

The school reflects community values. These values enter the school environment with and within the students—their dress, behavior, language, values, interests, attitudes, and sense of adolescent appropriateness.

Students want to be accepted, to belong. In school they generally will do what their group approves; they will refrain from whatever would cause group disapproval. Students want teachers to take charge. In every well-run class some if not most students are willing to cooperate with the teacher towards this end. **Sometimes the teacher may need to point out that this is in the students' best interest.**

In this section teachers share some of their many methods of taking charge. . . .

* * * * *

- The best preventive against discipline problems is a stimulating class, but keeping the class stimulating is, I believe, more difficult now than years ago because of TV and many societal changes. (21)
- If the entire class misbehaves I keep them all for a minute or so after the class exchange bell. (I note the administration doesn't like this method, though.) Occasionally, I pick the worst four of five students to keep after school. (11)
- Speak softly and individually to students; make them strain a little to hear. One of the class requirements is that each student is to bring good manners to class every day along with textbook and writing equipment. Speak clearly about expectations, listen to and watch student reactions. Sometimes just pose the question "Why?" then LISTEN. (31)
- Walk around the room — be visible. Simply standing beside disruptive students often ends misconduct, because they feel embarrassed and pressured. Let students know you respect them, like them, and care; in return they will respect you. The best discipline is a good lesson plan. DON'T BE PETTY. (13)
- I strive to use management techniques (starting on time, organized method for turning in and returning work, scheduling conferences, etc.) to help eliminate some discipline problems. I have policies I stick to, e.g. regarding hall passes. (40)
- A good rule is: Treat every student equally and give encouragement for any special effort or achievement. (28)
- To help empower students I teach them the "Pro and Con" technique for making decisions. I teach them also this 5-step decision-making strategy:
  1. Clarify the situation.
  2. Search for alternatives.
  3. Identify the criteria.
  4. Evaluate the alternatives and make decisions.
  5. Develop a plan of action and follow through.

These decision-making strategies are applicable generally, and useful in particular classroom situations including discussions related to student conduct and the common good. I emphasize each student's responsibility for his/her conduct; I strongly urge self-control as an effective sign of maturity. Sometimes, in good classes, students will check one another to keep class running smoothly. (35)

- I've struggled with this, like everyone else. Most of all, I try to be clear about my expectations regarding a learning environment. I talk clearly about respect for others and confront students who are disrespectful, rude, or disruptive. I have learned how to confront a student in a caring way, listening to what the student is saying verbally and non-verbally, since I've been involved in C.A.P.P.— Chemical Abuse Prevention Program. I've had good responses from whole classes and from individual students when I've been able to show some controlled anger and confront them. I make students responsible for their own actions. I'm having increasing support from the high school nurse and the counseling staff. The services provided by C.A.P.P. have been extremely helpful. (14)

- Keep classroom neat and orderly so that students, on entering the classroom will have an immediate impression of order. This influences behavior in a positive way. (25)

- Make sure all students are aware of rules. When a student doesn't follow through on rules, take necessary steps to correct the problem. Be consistent and fair. (22)

- Keep classroom rules few, fair, clear, enforceable. Give students responsibility for (a) being physically and mentally present daily, on time, and prepared for class, (b) controlling personal thoughts, words, and actions in favor of the common good of the entire class, (c) listening attentively and actively to the teacher and also to their classmates, (d) participating by asking relevant questions and volunteering answers, (e) fulfilling all requirements to the best of individual ability, (f) contributing to classroom harmony, teamwork and courtesy.

  In short, the student is expected to be a responsible and active participant in his/her learning process. (35)

- The 100 + page handbook, *Games Students Play (and what to do about them),* by Ken Ernst, (Celestial Arts, 231 Adrian Road, Millbrae, California 94030) adapts the techniques of Eric Berne to the classroom — (Berne is originator of Transactional Analysis, author of *Games People Play*).

  When a "game" prevents teaching, how does the teacher recognize and derail it? How turn the game off? *Games Students Play* suggests practical solutions to various practical problems many teachers encounter. (35)

- Social pressure works. Sort individual students out in front of class, if private conference is ineffective. Stress safety aspects; stress reasons for discipline; stress how all benefit; stress the attitude of self-reliance and self-control. (34)
- Rarely if ever discipline the entire class, because rarely is *everyone* guilty. Discipline an isolated individual in the hall. Discuss the purpose of the rule broken and determine why there was a behavior problem. Then firmly reestablish the student's responsibility to correct his/her behavior. (36)
- As a last resort for the whole class I have used a "Mitwirkungs-indexziffer" (participation index number) in an effort to curb unnecessary chatter. Every student gets a certain number of points added to his/her daily grade each day for a week if the class can control its noise level. On occasion, I have slammed my books on the desk and refused to teach when a class won't discipline itself. On the individual level, I try to negotiate the way to desired behavior outcomes rather than relying on a power play with a student. I don't "plea bargain," but I do insist that a student measure up to expectations he/she and I both have. A stone-like stare over the top of my glasses can work wonders. A short, "I want to see you after class" in the middle of a presentation, delivered without breaking stride, can make a point very quickly with a student. (27)
- I tell class, "Do not talk when anyone else is talking." They usually stop. Sometimes I change their seats. I explain how, as long as they behave, they can work together. If they abuse privileges, they lose rights: I become dictator. (6)
- I develop rapport with the group. I talk with and to misbehaving students individually, when possible. Unfortunately sometimes resort to anger seems necessary. (33)
- I **always** deal with **individuals.** It's easy to spot the insecure students who will test you and try to set up an adversarial relationship. I attempt to subvert that right away by giving those individuals special duties, attention. The most important aspect of maintaining discipline is absolute **fairness.** Students know that I **like** them all. (15)
- Standing outside the classroom door and greeting students with small talk and friendliness often gives the teacher an idea of "where they're coming from." Awareness of them as individual persons is the key. (18)

- When an extraordinary problem arises, I prefer immediate office reaction, but, since I haven't been getting that here, I occasionally pitch a "controlled fit" in that hour. I sometimes put a student outside the door, with individual settling of the matter to follow. Separate a pair (tell them "it's until the next day," conditional on their behavior). Usually a phone call to parents is effective.

  I tell students I prefer their self-control because I prefer to like them. I insist they listen while I talk, and I listen when they speak. I try to give students a few free minutes at the end of the hour. (18)

- Efficient classroom management provides a key to better use of teaching time as well as the quality of the student learning. Planning is essential. Be clear about expectations (academic, behavioral), about rules, and consequences. (26)

- Focus on successes, not failures. We cannot expect 100 percent of ourselves, nor of our students at all times. Allow for mistakes, for limitations. If we must find fault, we must be sure also to find reasons to praise. Try to make student success possible. (26)

- **Fear** will not motivate to goodness but rather to lie, to cheat, to sneak. **Love** will motivate to goodness. Trusting and respecting the student communicates love, as does patience, and an occasional going out of one's way. (26)

QUESTIONS FOR DISCUSSION

1. (a.) How does a teacher take and maintain control within the classroom? (b.) What is essential for control? Rank essentials.
2. "The best preventive against discipline problems is . . . " (21) p. 30. (a.) How do teachers today capture and maintain student interest in the subject? (b.) How do teachers make their subjects "come alive" for students? (c.) How do you make your subject "come alive," interesting, stimulating to students? Share your technique(s).
3. (a.) Is the ability to make classwork interesting, stimulating to students a gift? or can it be acquired? (b.) If it can be learned, how? where? from whom?
4. "Keep classroom neat and orderly . . . " (25), p. 31. (a.) How does a neat, orderly class contribute to classroom management? What are elements of order in a classroom? (b.) Discuss the effects of a disorderly classroom on procedures, on students, on the teacher.
5. For the first week of a new semester or year, many teachers seat class members alphabetically by last name. These teachers concentrate on learning names, faces, behaviors — to gain the necessary advantage. Do you have a better or different method? Share.
6. "The basis for teaching students to be responsible is making them aware of their behavior and its impact on others, then giving them an opportunity to correct the situation" (Duke and Meckel, 1984). (a.) Are students generally unaware of the effect of their behavior on others? (b.) How does a teacher give students an opportunity to correct the situation, then enforce the decision made?
7. "Make sure students are aware of rules . . . " (22), p. 31. (a.) What classroom rules are essential? (b.) How can students be involved in decision-making about rules and in their enforcement?
8. "Social pressure works . . . " (32), p. 32. How does a teacher exert social pressure in other ways? Give examples.

9. "Efficient classroom management provides a key . . . " (26), p. 33. Discuss.

10. "Resist beginnings. The prescription comes too late when the disease has gained strength by long delays" (Roman poet, Ovid). Paraphrase and apply this maxim to classroom management.

Phone Renewal
965-2595

Musical

Phone renewal service is available 24 hours a day, 7 days a week.

Your call renews items checked out to you that qualify for phone renewal *(See below for items that cannot be renewed.)* All current loan policies apply to phone renewals and any questions about loan policies should be directed to the staff of the Circulation desk.

- Write down and save the verification code word.
- When prompted give your name, ASU ID number and your daytime phone number.

New due date:

- You are responsible for knowing your new due date(s).
- Phone renewal will not inform you of your new due date(s). Call 543-8520 or check your account on-line after 48 hours to verify the renewal and obtain your new due dates.
- Renewable Law Library items may be renewed two (2) times only.
- Community Card borrowers may renew eligible items up to five (5) times each.

The following are not eligible for phone renewal:

- Materials checked out with special permission, such as Reference books.
- Materials recalled by another borrower.
- Materials from special departments (e.g., reserves, media, microforms).
- Materials obtained through Interlibrary Loan.
- Materials exceeding the maximum number of renewals.
- Items checked out to patrons who have library fees, expired ID, or otherwise currently suspended borrowing privileges.

• Besides having good relationships with the students, good teachers bring in new ideas and current articles to share with the class which most students enjoy greatly.

-Vince Johnston,
Howell High School, class of '85

4

• Report from a classroom, student explaining why he received four F's and one D on a report card: "I must have spent too much time on one subject."

CHAPTER 4

ON RAPPORT

AS CONSIDERED here, rapport implies an earned mutual respect and trust between the teacher and students, as well as between students. Rapport implies classroom harmony, cooperation, and concerted efforts towards established goals of the class. Because a harmonious class tolerates few disciplinary problems, teachers strive to achieve and maintain rapport with students—both in and out of the classroom.

Much depends on the teacher's personality, and the personalities of students. Experienced teachers suggest some methods they practice and find successful. Most emphasize the importance of greeting students by name as they enter the classroom, in the halls, and elsewhere. Many suggestions overlapped. In such cases, most repetitions were dropped to spare the reader.

* * * * *

- Students appreciate a teacher taking a personal interest in them. Questions like "How was the game last night?" "Is your mom feeling better now?" or "Did you get your car fixed yet?" tell a student that the teacher knows something about him or her beyond the classroom. I try to put myself in the student's place and say, after a particularly difficult presentation, "Yeah, I know, it doesn't seem to make any sense right now. You're wondering if you'll ever be able to do this, etc. . . . " They like to know you can feel for them. Sometimes it is necessary to break stride with a class and "let down your hair," or to confront them about something and get some interaction going, e.g. "Why do you think I've been unfair in asking this of you? Do you have a better way to do it?" (27)

- In dealing with students, individually and as a group, it is important to be sincere and honest. Share your feelings with them and also share personal experiences which relate to current issues under discussion. Do not condescend to students as if they were children, because they are young adults with developing independent thinking skills which teachers need to encourage. (23)

- Give students time to tell you how they feel. At mid-semester I give them a course evaluation and teacher evaluation—their expectations, assignments, methods, their effort. I encourage constructive comments. We discuss results. I send a progress report home to the parents of each student at least once a year, preferably the first quarter, with handwritten comments—something positive, along with negatives, as a rule. I often put my hand on a student's shoulder or back when working with them individually. (It is said that touching is therapeutic.) (6)

- I watch, listen, joke with students. I care and show it. This comes easily for me. Between classes and the first two or three minutes of class I talk to students and tease or tell a joke. I often relate personal experiences or ask for theirs. I compliment individuals or the class and compliment people on their dress, or test results, or an answer. Make the classroom "personalized." (8)

- Be fair, consistent, and firm, also respectful and interested. Accept the different personalities but never accept disrespect. Let the students know you are an individual also with likes and dislikes, special interests, responsibilities and so on. Share some of your every day experiences with them and they will see you as a total person. They often start showing an interest in you, as you do in them. (11)

- I try to call on every student during the hour to read off the answer(s) to an assignment if time allows. I call them by name and give them respectful attention and encouragement. (24)

- Ask students who understand the assignment or project to work with students who need a little more help. (25)

- I do much talking with students before and after class or after school about matters unrelated to my class. I ask questions about sports or other areas of their interest. During class I tease students, for example by "picking" on a few students who are capable of teasing back. When students see I can give and take jokes in a pleasant way, they usually are more comfortable with me. (22)
- I get student information at the beginning of each semester, and study it to learn about those I'll teach. I individualize as much as possible to allow each student to succeed at his/her level of ability. At the end of class I allow five minutes for individual questions or to carry on a short conversation relative to the class. I often ask students to contribute. (34)
- Some students comment on the importance of good student-teacher relationships. (Appendix, pp. 94)
- Calling a different parent every few days just to converse helps. They love to hear positive things, and later—if there is a problem—there is some background, and the report is better received. (30)
- I walk around the room while students are working on an assignment. I write comments on their work. Sometimes I ask why someone looks so sad or so happy. (7)
- It helps to be interested and enthusiastic about the subject you teach. I try also to be very well prepared. Return corrected papers promptly, to exhibit the type of behavior you expect of students. Try to be fair. Explain expectations clearly and also the grading system at the beginning of the term. (5)
- Recognizing students by name as they enter the classroom or when we meet in the hall is important. Also, going to some of their activities—sports events, dances, Pip-Fest—helps them see you as an interested, integrated person. Chatting with individual students about their interests and goals is good. Allowing the class as a whole to discuss their feelings on topics such as shoplifting, drinking, drugs, and other problems lets them know you are interested. It is, for the teacher, enlightening and sometimes frightening. (21) (Editor's Note: PIP-FEST: Partners in Prevention. Annual weekend at Howell High School for youth. Initiated and headed

by teachers and drug-abuse counselors, Ted Klontz and Margie Zugich. Support staff includes other teachers, administrators, parents, and other interested adults. Some community businesses contribute. Purpose: To help young people face and deal with their problems; to help young people prepare for a very demanding world; and to create and maintain a support system.)

- Praise students publicly; criticize privately. When teaching, look at every student. Wait until you have the attention of all. At other times, LISTEN, LISTEN, LISTEN. (31)

- I learn students' names the **first** week they are in my class. This is very important. When I have a minute before or after class I talk to students a bit about something they might be interested in. I call on them by name, often Mr. or Ms. or Miss, establishing a more formal yet comfortable academic environment. (19)

- Individual, visual eye contact with each student is my most effective method of establishing or beginning to establish rapport. I have found that, with the press of curriculum and time, if I stand at the door between classes and greet each student with a brief "hello" and call each by name, I establish personal eye contact and do much to build rapport. (20)

- My method is warmth, demonstrated in various ways—for example: appropriate strictness and respect; allowing humor; allowing students to be themselves; accepting them as they are; allowing students to work in groups or with a study partner as I walk around listening and caring, guiding as necessary. (10)

- In giving examples, I use students' names in fictional situations for humor or to make a point. For example: "You, John, have just been accused of murdering the postman by stuffing him in the mailbox for delivering a 'Dear John' letter. What are your rights?" (16)

- Every day I try to say something personal to each student. I move around the classroom. I find usually a touch or a stare can silence a misbehaving student more effectively than yelling. I try to compliment students on their appearance (hair cut, clothing, etc.), if I know they can handle that type of comment. I try to write positive comments and reactions on students' papers when appropriate. I make myself available after school to work with students who need additional help. I try to joke with students to get them working, rather than coming on strong, unless necessary. A smile can often defuse a potentially serious situation. I try to learn student names as soon as possible, and greet students in the hall or outside of school. Even after they are no longer in my class; I ask how their new classes are going. (17)

- I always try to treat students with the dignity and respect that every human deserves. I like to have stories that relate what we are studying to personal experiences of the students. (2)
- I teach and emphasize such concepts as the common good (group over student interests during class), class harmony (accord on goals and on means toward goals), teamwork (cooperation, working as individuals and as a group to achieve, to accomplish set purposes), self-control, rights of and responsibilities towards others as well as oneself.

  I try to recognize, praise, and encourage efforts and successes, and to downplay mistakes. (35)
- Walking around the classroom and talking with students on an individual basis during informal assignments is particularly effective for me. Letting students know there's a person who shares similar interests behind the authoratative figure we present is important. Be personally interested; show students you care. Students respect teachers who are competent. (9)
- Treat students with respect. Praise their creativity. Praise their performance. (33)
- Assign work which is challenging but which everyone can do at least partially — for early confidence. (4)
- The initial class assignments I give are somewhat personal, so I have a chance to discuss students' interests with them. When students are behind in homework I call parents; they know I care. I set up individual conferences with students during the class hour to discuss their progress. I use humor extensively and, I hope, appropriately. Even after reprimanding them, I return to being friendly. I try **never** to use sarcasm. Young people's egos are too fragile, and the teacher's role is powerful. Students know they can't fight the teacher, so inside anger can build up. We're helping them to grow. This requires care, time, and much patience. (18)

- Students seem to be interested in hearing about things you have done either at their age or at other points in your life. Occasional sharing some of these tends to make you appear more a person and less an authority symbol. (3)
- Rapport is mutual respect and understanding, to be developed with consistency and fairness. Individual attention between classes and after school strengthens rapport. I attend many school-related activities such as choral and band performances, and ball games. I mention these to students when appropriate. (39)
- I tend to have much interaction with students, even if it is a short exchange as they enter or leave the classroom. This takes regular effort, since I have equipment and supplies to put away and set up. We occasionally spend some class time listening to the concerns of each other, often in small groups. This helps students develop a sense of sharing, caring, and community, and also develops communication skills. I encourage students to share honestly, and to include suggestions for improving the course. (40)
- I try to tease, or to ask a question of a different student every day in each class. If I notice one looks extra sad, happy, worried, etc., I make a special effort to speak with this student about the reason for the evident emotions. By the end of the semester I have given personal attention to every student in my classes. It really makes a difference when a teacher talks to his/her students about the students' problems, interests, and ambitions. (30)
- My Health Occupations classes are somewhat smaller than others, so I can get to know students individually. We share in small groups as well as on a person-to-person basis, developing various personal and social qualities as part of Health Care skills. It's important that we address vital, real-life issues from the student's individual perspective as well as broader career implications. (14)
- In the drafting classes I usually greet each student at the door with his or her tape (for taping down work) and say "Hi" or "Howdy, _____." This helps also in taking attendance, and means students can commence work much faster.

    I try to learn of hobbies or interests the students have and then try to become at least moderately knowledgeable about that subject. Usually that isn't too difficult because most students like cars, music, and movies — the subjects I also enjoy.

During the class hour I walk around the room and make little comments on drawings, or remark if a student is doing well in a wrestling match, etc. To help them feel more at home in class, I try to make all comments in a positive, constructive, non-condescending manner. (29)

- I try to discuss students' interests with them. Often I go to events in which they are participating. I try to praise them whenever they deserve praise, and to keep an encouraging and positive attitude towards students. (37)

- I believe rapport is established by:

  1. Being yourself as well as the teacher (e.g. authentic, sincere, business-like, yet friendly and interested.)
  2. Listening both actively and reflectively.
  3. Having confidence in your decisions.
  4. Being firm and fair.
  5. Believing in your subject and your purpose as a teacher.
  6. Involving students in class participation and in some decision-making. (26)

- Over the years those teachers I've observed to have good rapport with students **never:**

  1. Attack a student verbally or otherwise.
  2. Use a classroom forum for pointing out individual weaknesses.
  3. Hold separate rules for different students.
  4. Talk down to students.

For interested teachers I recommend *Learning Discussion Skills Through Games.* (By Gene Standford and Barbara Dodds Standford. Available from Scholastic Magazines, Inc. 50 West 44th Street, New York, New York 10036.) (26)

QUESTIONS FOR DISCUSSION

1. Consult student comments: "Importance of Student-Teacher Relationships" (Appendix, p. 94). Discuss.

2. (a.) How is rapport achieved, earned? (b.) What human qualities in teachers and in students promote good relationships? (c.) What behaviors and activities . . . ?

3. Perfect rapport is not possible. (a.) What is ideal regarding teacher-student relationships in the classroom situation? (b.) What is realistic, desirable, acceptable? Discuss.

4. Teachers, as older and more experienced persons, have the greater responsibility to initiate, develop, and maintain rapport with students. (a.) What consistent attitudes, communications, interactions with students promote rapport? (b.) What is the responsibility of students? (c.) When necessary, how do teachers teach students this responsibility?

5. "Be fair, consistent, and firm." (11), p. 40. Do you agree these are valid norms? What would you add? or with what would you differ?

6. The question of appropriate humor and friendliness with students requires some reflection. Students are quick to spot and take advantage of what they perceive as weaknesses, affectation, eccentricity, lack of preparedness. How do teachers function in a business-like yet friendly manner?

7. "I teach and emphasize such concepts as . . . " (35), p. 43. (a.) In practical terms, how are such concepts taught? (b.) What is the value?

8. "I believe rapport is established by . . . " (26) p. 45. Do you agree? Can you add to the list? or improve it?

9. "Over the years those teachers . . . " (26), p. 45. Do you agree? Can you add to the list?

10. "I try to discuss . . . " (37), p. 45. (a.) How important is rapport between teachers in this school? between teachers and administrators? between teachers and students? (b.) Are we in control of our attitudes? How can we change our own or others' negative attitudes which prevent, damage, or destroy relationships?

- *The simplest kind of punishment is a reproof given to the student immediately after the fault. This is quick and almost painless. It helps form good habits by checking the bad ones in formation.*

  -Gilbert Highet,
  The Art of Teaching

5

- *Report from a classroom, student defending an unsatisfactory report card: "Well, look, I brang up my English mark, didn't I?"*

- *Report from a classroom, a discussion in civics: "The difference between a president and a king is that a king has no vice."*

CHAPTER 5

ON DISCIPLINE

TEACHERS WORK in various ways to encourage responsible student conduct, to prevent problem behavior. Preventive measures are important.

Effective classroom management together with earned rapport will significantly reduce the probability of student misbehavior. Even so, in the best of classrooms, unexpected, unwelcome problems do arise.

Good teachers stop negative behavior quickly. They communicate their perception of the problem to the student, and try to understand the student's perception. When possible, a fair settlement is negotiated, including insurance against recurrence of the problem. Some teachers use the situation as an opportunity to teach such concepts as cause and effect relations, responsibility, honesty, self-control. For students this can be an unusual learning experience. Many teachers emphasize effective measures such as a **private** conference or confrontation with the erring student outside the classroom. Without complete success, I tried to reduce repetitions, hoping to spare the reader.

(Incidentally, not one teacher made reference to the proverbial rod or hickory stick.)

This section does not deal with reasons for student misbehavior, numerous and sometimes complex as they are. Rather, we present preventive and corrective measures teachers use to help students take responsibility for their words and actions in the school community.

* * * * *

49

- Communicate clear expectations in both academic and behavioral areas. Students understand and judge these expectations as both reasonable and fair, accepting their own responsibility. Consistent, relentless enforcement of a few, fair, accepted rules is important. A genuine affection for the students helps immensely. (35)
- Presuming efficient classroom management which involves the students, and rapport with them (both attained with persistent effort), these are steps one can take:
  1. a disapproving glance directed steadily at the student who is "out of line;" if necessary, a second longer look;
  2. a short, pointed statement to the student (a quip or use of satire, but never sarcasm which could alienate);
  3. a serious discussion with the student in private. This usually suffices;
  4. a call to the parents. If step #3 does not work, this call usually does. In some cases I suggest a weekly report. This promotes cooperation between teacher-parent and either motivates or puts pressure on the student;
  5. a contract, signed by student, with a copy to each: parents, administrator in charge, and counselor (cf. pp. 57-59);
  6. rarely is it necessary to involve an assistant principal. However, this is a realistic and possible option.

  A good rule: resolve difficulties and problems at the lowest possible level. Respecting, being patient with high school students, treating them as young adults is usually effective — in class as well as in private discussion. Finding and praising good qualities improves attitudes and helps motivate good behavior and cooperation. (35)
- Pop quizzes can be effective to activate the class promptly, thus cutting down on or eliminating potential disruptions. (24)
- Send progress reports home whenever a problem arises, rather than waiting for scheduled dates (mid-quarter or report cards). Isolate the disruptive student: put him/her in the hall with assigned work. (4)
- I take away planned video-material privileges and substitute written work which the particular class does not like as a penalty for general misconduct. (37)

- I talk to the students individually. I'm not afraid to let them know when I'm upset or disappointed. I don't confront upset students too directly or aggressively, but diffuse the situation promptly—and then talk with them. (19)
- I use an approach I refer to as the "tick" system. Each time a student misbehaves I put a mark beside his/her name in my grade book. When they reach three ticks, I issue an hour detention after school. For the second three ticks the student receives two hours detention, etc. I detail the kind of behavior I consider inappropriate when the system is initiated. It provides some give and take, but—if I want—a student can accumulate ticks very quickly. Most become very conscious of the resulting consequences when I simply reach for my gradebook during class. The result is this: they stop misbehavior, and I usually don't even have to raise my voice. A look will usually suffice. (17)
- Catching the problem early, and verbally dealing with the student on a one-to-one basis is effective. Letting the student know his/her behavior is inappropriate in your classroom is a big priority. Students face six different teachers every day. What is allowed in one class is forbidden in the next. Students need to know where the line is in your class.

  I limit hall passes to one per semester for each student. I simply place a "done" by the student's name in my attendance book and check before I write passes. This cuts down on most of the abuses. (9)
- I do not hesitate to call parents for even a minor situation. This is because I make an effort to call for positive things as well. I make approximately four calls to different parents each week. I rarely write referrals. If the situation is questionable I will discipline a student for using poor judgment in a situation. Usually, I require the student(s) to serve detentions with me or I assign some other appropriate discipline related to the situation. (40)
- I keep the student in the classroom after other students have left and talk with him/her. I have students clean the classroom after school to compensate for disrupting class or for breaking classroom rules. (37)

- Discipline should be dealt with by the teacher. Only as a last resort, when all seemingly reasonable methods fail, do I refer students to higher authority. (29)
- I set up an individual conference with a student when necessary. By praising good students, I use the peer pressure of mature behavior. Sometimes immediate verbal reprimands are called for. A conference with an administrator, parents, and the student is needed to resolve some situations. (10)
- I talk to the individual, and attempt to get the student to agree about what is acceptable behavior and why rules are necessary. Confront the most difficult individuals. Keep the class working on assignments. Walk around to assure desired appropriate use of class time. (5)
- Over the years, I have found discipline to be most successful when:

  1. I don't take misconduct personally and don't make quick assumptions;
  2. I realize something else has triggered this behavior, e.g.
     a. Problems at home
     b. Personal problems
     c. Poor nutrition
     d. Over-tired because of an outside job, or another reason;
  3. I deal with this problem on an individual level, quietly;
  4. I show little anger (yelling, screaming); rather I talk logically with the student(s) causing them to give reason(s) for what was said or done. When I ask "why?" I'm often amazed to discover the real cause of the problem. (30)

- It's best not to be afraid to FACE a problem with a student. I talk to the student; I ask him/her to talk with me about the problem. Often they know of no better way to respond to situations. I practice the Golden Rule on these young people. I try to teach them that there is always a better way to achieve and to solve problems. (30)
- My first step is to talk to the student privately outside the classroom or quietly at his/her desk; then, if possible, I choose him/her to work on some classroom project. This often helps change

a negative attitude. When necessary, I try to discuss the problem with parents and get their approval on keeping the student after school the same day he/she acts up. Finally, if all else fails, I refer to the assistant principal. (11)

- Giving a student a leadership role often precludes disruptive behavior. Move troublesome students closer to the teacher's desk. (2)

    Assertive Discipline techniques are good. Classroom rules are posted along with consequences for ignoring or violating them. This discipline policy progresses from talking with the student; with his/her parents; then a teacher-student session after school; detentions; and, finally, referral to the appropriate principal. With individual students who don't understand, or who have a hard time following assigned procedures, I have a classroom contract discussed and designed by both student and teacher. The contract is short term for quick accomplishment and reward. For one week, the assignment and student conduct is checked on a log dated and signed by the student each day. This gives me the opportunity to recognize daily academic effort and improved conduct. Usually after a week or several, the student can continue on his/her own. If not, the contract is rewritten and the log required again. (38)

- In an after school detention with me, the student must do assigned book work. (25)

- Remove the disruptive student from the class and talk to him/her individually. Have a student-teacher conference at lunch time. I do not allow the student in my next class unless he/she comes to talk with me about modifying his/her behavior. Calling parents is often effective. Isolate individuals as "sacrificial lambs." (8)

- When I have a discipline problem with an individual student, I go over to his/her desk and ask this student to see me after class. At this point I will reason with the student, being as open and honest as possible. I listen carefully to statements and responses. We come to terms acceptable to both of us. (23)

- Discipline works best when prompt and fair. I try to avoid letting a student paint himself into a corner where he feels he has no alternative. I explain why what he did is causing a problem with the operation of the class. (3)

- One-to-one private conversations about the infraction works best for me. I try to get the individual student to acknowledge his/her misconduct and to agree to terms to remedy the problem. (22)
- After I talk with the student I may call the parent, assign detention, and as a last resort write a referral to the assistant principal in charge. If the entire class is involved: bribery. (21)
- If a student causes trouble I assign an after-school detention with me to permit that student to make amends. (7)
- I strive to be sure that students know I care about them as persons before I discipline them. When there is a problem I follow these steps:

  1. I address the student and discuss the incident to see if we have a misunderstanding about expectations.
  2. I contact the student's parents if the problem recurs.
  3. Then, if the problem continues, I send him to the assistant principal's office for appropriate next steps.

  Often the disruptive student has a home problem which manifests itself in school. If I can avoid a confrontation, counseling is often better than a more severe course of action. (39)
- First I talk with the disruptive student. Then 75-80 percent of the time a call home will take care of whatever problem exists. My next step is to contact the counselor or the appropriate assistant principal or both. (24)
- I let students know my limits before an incident happens. Then the first time anything (even small) bugs me they understand my facial expression, vocal tone, and choice of words. (40)
- It is my opinion that teacher education programs should include an intensive course in dealing with severe behavior problems, including strategies for classroom management.

  1. **Do** discipline specific behavior. **Do not** attack the person for his/her behavior.
  2. **Do** involve significant others including parents, fellow teachers, counselors, administrators. **Do not** avoid such contact, fearing admission is a sign of weakness.
  3. **Do** put all discipline in a context of positive reinforcement leading to desired goals.

4. **Do** adhere to the school code of conduct policies. **Do not** seek to earn student allegiance through leniency or stretching of established limits.
5. **Do** discipline all students equally and fairly. **Do not** single out trouble makers by labeling. **Do not** play favorites.
6. Finally, **do be consistent.** (26)

TYPICAL SCHOOL FORMS

(as referred to by teachers in Chapter 5)

_____ HIGH SCHOOL
DETENTION NOTICE
                                          Date   _____
_____   Grade   _____
Student's Name
Is assigned detention on the following dates:

_____
Remarks: _____
_____
_____

Served: Date(s)   _____ _____ _____ _____
No Show: Date(s)   _____ _____ _____ _____

_____   _____
Referring Teacher's Signature   Detention Teacher's Signature

_____   _____
Student's Signature   Administrator's Signature

S 10-A   White: Assistant Principal, then student file
         Pink: Detention Teacher   Yellow: Referring Teacher
         Goldenrod: Student

- -

DISCIPLINE REPORT
                                          Date _____
Teacher Name _____
Student Name _____
Class _____ Room #_____
Hour _____
Please complete the information below. Be as objective, factual, and detailed as possible. This informa-
tion will be extremely valuable in communicating with the student and parents.
Briefly describe the incident(s)   Date of incident(s) _____
_____
_____

Give supporting facts: _____
_____
_____
_____
_____

Original: Teacher   Pink: Assistant Principal   Yellow: File

- -

SUSPENSION NOTICE
DATE:
NAME: AGE:
REASON FOR SUSPENSION:

PERIOD OF SUSPENSION:
NOTIFICATION OF PARENT: (phone or Letter)
TIME AND DATE OF PARENT CONFERENCE:
                    PRINCIPAL'S SIGNATURE _____
REMARKS AND CONDITIONS:
ANY ADDITIONAL INFORMATION:
CENTRAL OFFICE RECEIVED: BOARD NOTIFIED: _____
S-5 White - Counselor   Yellow - Parent   Pink - Personnel
                          Goldenrod - Assistant Principal

STUDENT-TEACHER CONTRACTS

- To provide a wayward student an alternative to impending suspension or even expulsion, when appropriate and the student is responsive, a teacher may initiate a Student-Teacher Contract.

  Such a contract is more formal and binding than familiar teacher-student agreements, and more effective. Used with great care and rarely, it brings results. It saves time for the teacher, counselor or administrator, and parents. It also preserves respect for this formal last recourse before possible more severe action.

Steps:

1. The teacher initiates a conference with the student to discuss the student's predicament, and possible measures which school policy allows in such cases. The teacher informs the student of an option: the Student-Teacher Contract. The teacher also explains benefits and costs to the student. The student will assent because he/she understands the contract is intended to help.
2. The teacher tailors the contract in the name of the particular student. It states the specific inappropriate conduct, and promises the student's self-correction and self-control. Even when reluctant to go through with it a student will prefer this option to impending more severe measures.
3. The teacher describes the matter, in confidence, with the appropriate counselor or administrator, and schedules a meeting, to include this school official, in his or her office.
4. The teacher informs the parents of the need, purpose, time and place of the meeting, and invites them. Parents welcome the positive, supportive approach; always one or both is/are present at the meeting.
5. The meeting of teacher, counselor or administrator, parent(s), and the student can be pleasant, but its purpose is serious, as all — especially the student — understand.

   The teacher states the problem; the student acknowledges it. Others present may contribute to the discussion. In the end, the student reads the contract aloud, acknowledges it as fair and reasonable, then signs it. The original is filed in the office; parents and students each receive a copy. The teacher also keeps one, in case a reminder is ever necessary. The student will conform, despite occasional difficulty, because it is in his/her interest to do so, and he/she feels bound by the contract.

Effective teachers know that high school students need to be treated with respect. The Student Teacher Contract helps the student retain his/her dignity, correct the specific problems/behavior, and assume responsibility for personal actions in a more mature way. (cf. p. 50 #5). (35)

STUDENT-TEACHER CONTRACT: MODEL 1.

TO: (teacher) _____

FROM: (student) _____

ABOUT: _____

DATE: _____

I, _____ need the _____(course) credit (_____semester). I understand my obligation to improve my grade from a current _____ to _____ by _____.

Therefore I resolve daily to:

1. attend class on time, both mentally and physically;
2. pay attention to the teacher and to class work;
3. complete all assigned work on time, to the best of my ability;
4. participate appropriately in class;
5. control my behavior without teacher intervention; I will not talk out nor laugh nor act in any other way to distract myself or my classmates. I will not disrupt the class.
6. I will cooperate with the teacher and the on-going processes of the class. I will stay in my assigned seat during class.
7. I will study for and successfully pass quizzes, tests, and the final examination in the class.

I accept the teacher's warning that I will lose points any time I fail in my responsibility to comply with the terms of this contract.

I understand that by complying with this contract I will pass the class and earn the credit I need.

I will do my best to fulfill my obligations in this _____ class.

_____
(student signature)

copies: parents
        assistant principal
        counselor

STUDENT-TEACHER CONTRACT: MODEL 2.

TO: (teacher) _____

FROM: (student) _____

ABOUT: _____

DATE: _____

I, _____, realize that I need a high school diploma to make my way in life.

During my _____ year I have made some poor decisions. I have acted and spoken sometimes with little sense of personal responsibility. I have annoyed some of my teachers and class-mates. I have disappointed my parents. So far I have wasted some opportunities to gain a proper high school education.

Now I understand better that my words, actions and decisions have consequences. I could be ex-pelled from school.

From now on and during my _____ year, if the school gives me this chance I need:

I will be present, on time, daily;

I will be prepared for class, with completed homework, books and materials, and a positive attitude;

I will cooperate with my teachers, and I will do assigned work in every class as well as I can;

I will be a self-controlled young man/woman, and I will do my best to do the right thing—**thinking first** so my words and actions will be good.

and NO Discipline Referrals!

_____
(student signature)

copies to parents
      assistant principal
      counselor

QUESTIONS FOR DISCUSSION

1. "A good offense is the best defense." Apply this maxim, often heard in the sports world, to the classroom. Discuss.

2. "I **always** deal with **individuals.** It's easy to spot insecure students . . . " (15), p. 32. The teacher quoted shares an example of prompt identification of a potential problem, and positive action taken immediately to "subvert" it. Give other examples.

3. (a.) What do you expect and require of students regarding compliance with rules, and general classroom cooperation? (b.) How do you elicit the good will of students? (c.) How do you involve students to make them responsible for their own conduct and to gain their cooperation in maintenance of classroom order?

4. "The simplest kind of punishment is a reproof given to the student immediately after the offense. This is quick and relatively painless. It helps form good habits by checking bad habits in formation" (*The Art of Teaching,* Highet, 1950). Is this true today? Discuss.

5. "As hard as it is for me to say, I think a good teacher should give homework and press students to do it. It's the only way to get the material to stick in" (cf. Appendix, p. 94). Intellectual discipline can and must be taught. How? Discuss.

6. "Catching the problem early . . . " (9), p. 51. Students, and teachers as well, need to be adaptable, tolerant, understanding, at times forgiving. (a.) Could teachers agree on classroom rules to provide more consistency for students? How? (b.) Or is it necessary to retain individual classroom guidelines and rules? Why? Discuss.

7. "It is my opinion that teacher education courses should . . . " (26), p. 54-55. Discuss each of the six propositions.

8. Reflect on this standard policy of many teachers: Resolve ordinary problems at the lowest level. When necessary, take further steps. Settle the difficulty without outside help as a rule. Keep classroom control; 'power' slips out otherwise, while students observe and pass judgment. Discuss.

9. "To reinforce skills taught, he/she takes time in correcting and grading (A, B, C, etc.), returns papers promptly, and requires students to rewrite poor papers." (cf. Appendix, p. 93). Discuss methods.

10. Good teachers expect much of students; good students expect much of teachers. Discuss.

• *Organization requires a form of self-discipline. When a teacher is organized, class begins on time, thus reducing the potential for disorderly conduct in the classroom.*

-Susan Strong,
Howell High School, Class of '85

6

• *Report from a classroom, a history quiz: "The Civil War was caused by Lincoln signing the Emasculation Proclamation."*

CHAPTER 6

ON ORGANIZATION

MANY STUDENT behavior problems can be prevented. In this section we share techniques, methods of planning, organizing — using time and efforts well. Students know when the teacher has an organized plan and goals for the class. Students prefer order to its opposite — disorder. Students behave better in a well-organized class.

Planning ahead, organizing, gives direction to the day, to each class. Careful thought, careful planning, is essential.

Setting priorities, then communicating plans in outline form gives everyone an advantage. With a good plan, one can work without anxiety in the present — concentrating energies and talents on the task at hand.

The teacher who takes the time to organize well has more time, makes his/her work easier, and can work efficiently, effectively, and with self-confidence.

*****

- I have each student put his/her row number on all papers so that assignments can be recorded and handed back rapidly. I use a handmade alphabetizer for students to place papers in so that recording is faster. I often hand out a weekly lesson plan to the students so they know exactly what will be covered each day. (11)
- I use computer educational software. I put some responsibility on students to maintain individual files. (34)

65

- This method works for me:
  1. regularly preview all newly written and video materials;
  2. collect and organize current newspaper and magazine articles relevant to course work I teach;
  3. collect and classify video materials appropriate to each unit;
  4. organize all of the above in a three-ring binder, classified by topic;
  5. develop new tests or make current all other tests used for each topic.

  I repeat steps 1-5 every year. In the process of reviewing and researching, I usually find materials to expand the curriculum by creating new units to add to those I currently teach. Since the behavioral sciences are dynamic in nature, I must be also. (39)
- Use color coding. Different colors designate test grades, quizzes, assignments, projects, and also different time periods. (21)
- I grade on a number system and use a GRADEMATIC 100tm hand-held calculator. (Source: Calculated Industries, Inc., 2010 N. Tustin Avenue, Suite B, Orange, CA 92665, 1-800-854-8075. $29.95 in October, 1984). This practice saves time at progress report and report card times. It is easy, accurate and fair. (35)
- By the end of each hour, I try to check papers in so that I won't have to do a stack at the end of the day; otherwise a person would be swamped with too many papers at once. (24)
- It is important to keep records of all transactions with parents and subsequent actions with their son/daughter for future reference. Use a small 4 × 6 card file. Each student fills in his/her demographic information on one side at the beginning of the year. I note all transactions throughout the year on the back of each card. (23)
- By recording daily work with a symbol (✔+, ✔, ✔-, or 0), I can check it in quickly. I convert the symbol to a letter grade or to points when I correct each student's work. I record quizzes and tests in letter grades or points. I plan ahead by unit or by week and give a vocabulary quiz every Friday. Consequently,

students have no homework Thursday except to study for the scheduled quiz. I vary Friday lesson plans to keep students interested and to use class time well. (31)

- I fill out a calendar of the school year with all one-half days, parents' conference schedules, assemblies, quarter and semester-end exams and dates, etc. . . . I post the current month and one month in advance so both students and teacher are constantly reminded of "special" day schedules. (32)

- In our complex profession, organization is essential but often difficult. In teaching, I often focus on one or two objectives, then assign written work. When students submit their work I check papers in, then return them. Students exchange papers, circling any mistakes relative to the objective(s) I taught. Papers with over three mistakes must be re-written and re-submitted to me. In this way I eliminate some unnecessary paper-work for me, and students benefit also in the process. (30)

- I write fresh lesson plans every single day, so students can flip through and see what we did on any day they might have been absent. It adds continuity to my daily schedule, and students want to believe that what we do in the classroom is really all connected. Keeping records can be a chore unless they are updated daily and running totals are kept. (27)

- Since many language exercises have stock answers and students correct their own, it isn't necessary to collect them. I take two minutes at the beginning of class to check to see if assignment is complete. That way, students can't fill in answers while we check. I record missing or incomplete assignments later. Later (in 10 seconds) I fill in points for all the other students. (6)

- Use 3 × 5 cards as reminders and 8 × 11 pads of paper for planning each day's work. (8)

- Each student has a number—the number next to his/her name in my grade book. They are assigned to put it on all papers they turn in. This allows papers to be alphabetized very quickly. A student does this with homework while I take attendance, etc. (16)

- I write numbers, not grades, to record exams as this is more exact and fair. In history and social studies classes, on the first day of class I give the students reading assignments for the entire semester. Students appreciate knowing what is expected, and the policy saves much class time. Students are treated maturely. And we finish the book. (19)

- Even though we are not required to keep lesson plans, I keep a basic sketch of what I plan to cover each day. I write that in advance every Friday. If the plan is new, or I have dramatically modified an existing plan, I closely detail what I am planning. Sometimes I even write the time I believe the individual activities will take. In writing classes I try to complete each day's plan with an assignment several minutes before the end of the period. Students can then begin their work and there is time for questions if the assignment was not clear. At the start of each class period, I review the previous day's work as a carryover to new materials covered in class. (17)

- I use an in-basket approach to dealing with paperwork. I try not to touch most items more than once. When I first read a request, paper, etc., I try to respond. I then put this where I can get it to the sender as soon as possible. Once I have written the response, I usually don't have to think about it again. I use various tactics in composition class for dealing with the paper load, but that is another topic. I keep one calendar with all my appointments for school and outside activities listed. I look at it each evening before retiring. (17)

- I keep my grades on a computer. Once a week I add new grades (points) and run a copy of the class grades. I distribute this to students the next day so they know on a weekly basis what grade they are receiving and what work is missing. I don't believe in surprises when it comes to the grade a student earns. I keep a back-up disk in case the original program is lost. Before adding grades on a disk, I record them daily in my gradebook. This is another backup to the computer program. (17)

- I place a file holder on my desk and either label folders with class hours or use colored folders to distinguish each. I keep note paper clipped to the record book as a reminder of things to do, students to notice or contact. I put daily plans on the blackboard to eliminate confusion and the ever-ready question, "What are we going to do in here today?" (13)

- Each day I take home only the number of papers I can correct in one evening. When one sets an attainable goal, one can feel good about oneself. Motivation is easier when one is realistic about one's strengths and limitations. I have an "easy grader" which I purchased. I keep a file box of names and phone numbers (students' parents) for use when necessary. I keep a record of phone calls and of disciplinary problems, actions taken, and problem resolutions. (13) (Editor's Note: Easy grader: a cardboard, slotted chart with grade conversions, percentiles, etc., available at some book stores or teacher supply stores.)

- I keep the lesson plan book on my desk open to the page for next day so I can jot down things to remember to do tomorrow as they come to me. (33)

- Students keep their work in individual files which include pre-testing and post-testing, and student's written assignments. Copies of work belong in room. I use a variety of methods to reinforce learning of basic skills in language (dictation, lecture, guest speakers). Paper work is handled immediately but centers around a set of priorities. (10)

- When grading papers, I keep a clock in front of me and allot a given amount of time to each paper—then stick to it. I keep a ditto class list for each class, to use for recording book numbers of supplemental assigned books, individual book title choices for quarterly reading, field trip permission slips, etc. Then the gradebook doesn't become cluttered. (15)

- I record names in the gradebook to match attendance book numbers. Then, when I record grades, I know if students were absent or tardy. A circle in the box ⓪ indicates an assigned paper not turned in although the student is present; a square within the square ▣ in the gradebook indicates absence. In the gradebook I use percentages rather than letters. I fill in all spaces with 0-100 so I can add easier. At progress report time I place half-way totals. At semester time I add second quarter grades to the first. This method saves time at grading time. I divide the total points earned into 10 segments, and use the top 10 percent for A, etc. (18)

- I come in early when it is "quiet" to be sure everything is set before the first student arrives. I grade and return papers promptly so students receive them back the day after I picked them up. (3)

- Don't allow assignments and correspondence to stack up. (I'm still working on this one.) (12)
- I keep timelines for "assignments due" taped to desk for quick student reference. All assignments are written on board for students to copy. "Assignments completed" check list or "thermometer" also is on board for motivation of students and record keeping for teacher. (2)
- I keep a note slip or file card taped on my desk corner recording the page and location for reading or other work for each class next day. Here also I keep an outline lesson plan briefly stating what is to be covered. (4)
- The best technique I've found for organizing a teaching topic is to put it in a three-ring binder. This allows me to:
  1. add or delete material easily;
  2. have a record of all relevant hand-outs, tests, A-V materials, etc., in my file so that I don't forget some particular thing due to the volume of material covered;
  3. change/improve the order of the unit without rewriting it. (39)
- I maintain a notebook for the use of the occasional substitute teacher. It contains general information: name of school, schedule, attendance policy, lunch procedure, phone numbers, names and location of assisting teachers, etc. I add only the specific lesson plans that apply for the day I cannot be present. (40)
- Daily assignment checking and passing back and forth of papers can take class time. I keep a three-ringed notebook for the Algebra I class. Daily I check up and down the rows to spot completed or missing assignments. I record a zero for missing assignments. Then I read the correct answers so students can check their work. If a number of students miss the same problem(s), I re-teach, explain, answer questions, give examples, ask students to work out a problem on the board and to explain his/her work. Each student keeps all assignments intact to study for quizzes and tests. I collect the notebooks and grade them every two weeks. (38)

- I do not use class time to give make-up work. In my classes students understand they must see me before or after school to make up quizzes or tests because each member of every class, the whole class, deserves my total attention during class time. (40)
- I try to avoid unnecessary practices which could take away from class time tasks. On my own time I try to keep up with the great flow of paper. (29)
- I'm generally an organized person but I find organizing school work and materials a constant battle. Reorganizing a filing cabinet on a yearly basis is crucial. I've been challenged by development of the Health Education Curriculum — an ongoing process. Of primary importance, I've found, is a realistic balance between what's possible, what's crucial, and what's appealing. The challenge is to be in step with what's going on school-wide, the calendar, and individually, with both myself and the students. In Health Occupations and Health Education it's important to be responsive to major health issues. I will change plans to accommodate plans to what's happening. (14)
- At the semester beginning I have class members sign a sheet listing the class hour and the number of the book he/she will use. Then I post this sheet inside the cabinet where books are stored. A responsible student collects books each hour and reports daily any discrepancies. (37)
- Teachers must operate on the maxim: "THOSE WHO FAIL TO PLAN, PLAN TO FAIL."
  Planning should include the following:
  1. Daily lesson plan.
  2. Detailed unit plans which include goals and objectives, materials to be used, required A-V aides, texts, and supplementary materials needed.
  3. Long range plans outlining the expected curriculum from September to June. These must adhere to established district-wide plans. (26)
- For teachers of reading-writing oriented subjects, I highly recommend the text *How To Handle The Paper Load.* Several time-saving ideas are therein presented. (Publisher: National Coun-

cil of Teachers of English. 1111 Kenyon Road. Urbana, Illinois 61801. $7.00 in 1984). All teachers will be helped by availing themselves of computer assisted record-keeping strategies. Always operate on this basis: Keep teaching simple, clear, and direct. (26)

- Selected notes for teacher use from a conference: "Getting Things Done." Sponsored by Career Track, of Boulder, Colorado, in Ann Arbor, 9/13/85. Presenter: Bob Miller. Participants: 350 professional men and women.

1. Ground rules: Be prepared. Start on time. Relax, enjoy. Ask students to take notes, to ask questions, to think, to reflect, to express own ideas/views. Move toward pre-set objectives.

2. A person can hold only one conscious thought at a time. One's disciplined attention is only in one place at a time.

3. One cannot borrow, save, or buy time. The time one has is now. Be present to the present. "Live in the gladness of today."

4. The thought one holds determines one's behavior. Control of behavior comes from within, based on what one is thinking and feeling in the environment. Classroom environment affects students.

5. Set goals to achieve. Without goals one cannot evaluate what one is doing now.

6. Priority-setting system:

A. High	1. Importance
B. Medium	2. Urgency
C. Low	3. Growth

IMPORTANCE

	High Do it now.	Reports, routine trivia we do.
Urgency		
	Low Opportunity here, but no time pressure	Busy work, e.g. cleaning of desk, shuffling papers

1. How important, serious? A., B., C.?
2. How urgent? A., B., C.?
3. How growing? — If "A.," this alligator is getting out of control!

7. Urgency sets us in action to achieve goals.
8. Achievement requires goal-setting and focusing, time, dedication, energy, determination, and progressive evaluation.
   Know what you want.
   Know why you want it._
   Know when you want it.
   Know how you are going to get it.
   Begin immediately to get it (small steps).
   Monitor progress of activities and accomplishments.
9. "If you don't know where you're going, you'll probably end up somewhere else."
10. Teachers who manage by walking around (MBWA) use a tested and proven procedure of excellent management.

IMPROVING COMMUNICATION

1. Clarify objectives, purposes, goals.
2. KISS: keep it short and simple. Re-state when necessary.
3. Invite questions. Encourage students to think reflectively, not just memorize. Listen carefully. Respond.
4. Identify action steps: who is to do what? by when? and how?
5. Make sure students understand.
6. Have clear understanding up front. Let students know their responsibilities and constraints, rewards and penalties.

TWENTY-FIVE TIME-SAVING TIPS

1. Rewrite your goals and activities, and reprioritize them at least every three months.
2. Make a **daily** "To-Do-List" of activities which you need to accomplish.
3. Learn to say "No!" You need your time to work on your high-priority needs.
4. Assess routine activities in which you are involved; can any be eliminated or delegated?
5. Carry blank 3 × 5 cards on which you can make notes of things to remember.
6. Work on only one item at a time.

7. Provide adequate instructions — time is lost if a job is done incorrectly.
8. Train others to do jobs. You cannot do them all nor can others do them if they have not been trained.
9. Expect others to succeed; it becomes a self-fulfilling prophecy.
10. Help others see how they benefit from doing a job . . . when they become motivated.
11. Do not avoid talking with a poor performer. It hurts him/her, the organization, and yourself if the current matter is not given proper attention.
12. Don't over-control others — it's frustrating for them and time-consuming for you.
13. Focus on results of others, not activities or personalities.
14. Reward based on results produced.
15. Solve problems. Don't just fight fires.
16. If students are provided with feedback on their actual performance as compared to expected performance, they will tend to correct their own deficiencies.
17. Take classes to stay current in your field. The world is changing rapidly and you must learn to manage change or accept obsolescence.
18. Avoid losing your temper. Problems are not solved during emotional battles.
19. Finish what you start.
20. Attempting too much means spreading yourself too thin and failing to do an effective job.
21. Force yourself to plan.
22. Utilize waiting time. Read a book, plan your next day, work on a report or read your 3 × 5 cards.
23. Avoid worry. The majority of the things we worry about never occur.
24. Relax on weekends. You will return to school refreshed.
25. DO IT NOW! Don't procrastinate. (35)

*****

- Early in new courses, all students in my classes supply requested data—name, address, telephone number—on my Student Record form. I file these forms alphabetically by class hour in a ring-binder.

During the year I enter sketchy, positive notes for most students. For students with problems who cause problems I keep careful account of exact words, actions, dates—and measures taken to resolve the problem.

This Student Record serves when I need to call a parent, during parent-teacher conferences as a supplement to other records, and during teacher-student conferences. Often the record helps motivate a student to perform better academically or in conduct. (Model, below) (35)

_____HIGH SCHOOL .... ■ Student Record

SCHOOL YEAR: _____ SEM _____

Class Hour	Name:_____Age____DOB_____
_____ Grade	Address:_____Phone_____

Business phone for Father_____
Mother_____
Guardian_____

■ACADEMIC ACHIEVEMENT	■CONDUCT, COOPERATION, RESPECT

QUESTIONS FOR DISCUSSION

1. Many proven methods for using time well are shared in this book. (a.) What entries provide practical ideas you can use? (b.) List other ways to improve classroom efficiency.

2. How do you organize, label, and file materials, records, forms, data, so that, at any moment, you can locate whatever may be needed?

3. At class exchange time how do teachers manage to conclude a class, "be there" for students who approach after class, prepare for the next class, **and** stand in the hall to observe and greet students passing by as well as those entering the classroom? Discuss.

4. How do we teach students respect for themselves and others, for education, for class time, opportunities, activities, for rights of all class members, for school materials and properties? Discuss methods.

5. A. How do teachers enforce observance of respect and related obligations (cf. #4 above). How does observance of these duties help protect the rights of all class members, and promote good classroom management and organization?

6. (a.) What can students contribute to classroom management and organization? (b.) What can students do to assist teachers in selected classroom functions? (c.) What can teachers do towards leadership-training in the classroom? For example: students can lead group or general discussions; students can prepare and present reports to the class; students can take roles in simulation games cf. (31), p. 19. Discuss other examples.

7. What method do you use to help students who, because of absence, have missed presentations, assignments, quizzes and tests? How do you record transactions?

8. Some students have more problems, and create more problems than others. How do you keep record of problematic behavior and effective measures taken? Share.

9. In *Chalk Talks* teachers have shared many useful techniques. Can you add techniques you find useful?

10. For reflection . . .

"One ought every day at least
to hear a little song, read a good
poem, see a fine picture, and
if it were possible, to speak
a few reasonable words."

-Goethe

• *One of the most important qualities of a good teacher is humor. Many are the purposes it serves. The most obvious one is that it keeps the students alive and attentive because they are never quite sure what is coming next.*

  -Gilbert Highet,
  The Art of Teaching

• *Finish each day and be done with it. You have done what you could; some blunders and absurdities no doubt crept in; forget them as soon as you can. Tomorrow is a new day; you shall begin it well and serenely.*

  -Ralph Waldo Emerson

7

• *Report from a classroom: "I asked one student what he wanted to be when he grew up. He thought a long moment and then said, 'Alive.' "*

CHAPTER 7

A BIT OF THIS 'N THAT

I AM REMINDED of the French writer Charles Peguy's statement at the end of a particularly long letter: "Forgive the length of this letter, my friend. Had I had more time it would have been much shorter."

On the contrary, if teachers had more time, this chapter and others of *Chalk Talks* could have been much **longer**. The real strengths — knowledge and experience — to share, abide in our minds, hearts, wills, lives. With determination, with dedication we make every effort to provide for our students the most effective education possible. We appreciate shared leadership, team work, administrative support. We recognize and appreciate the abilities, qualities, and potential of our students. We are grateful for all who appreciate us and who support education especially in our own schools.

Teaching high school students is a challenge and a privilege. We contribute to their educational formation and foundation, to the on-going process of their life-long education and citizenship. This is the challenge. The privilege: "a teacher affects eternity; he can never tell where his influence stops." — (Henry Adams-The Education of Henry Adams. 1907).

* * * * *

• Have students help other students. If someone finishes early, have him/her answer other students' questions. Use visual materials, extensive chalk board diagrams, bulletin board displays. Display students' work (themes) with teacher's comments written on the paper so many can benefit. Send letter to parents of good students encouraging the student to take additional classes in the subject. Always send progress reports to keep parents informed. Include positive comments. (4)

- Invite community members and parents into certain classroom sessions and to Talent-a-Rama. Concentrate on positive aspects as well as on responsibilities of the teaching profession. (34)
- Making phone calls to parents regarding both behavior and lack of student work has been of help to me. (7)
- Expect mature behavior and thought. Students seem to live up or down to your expectations. (3)
- Keep expectations within the abilities of the individual. (12)
- Don't hand out copies at a staff meeting, and then read the material to the group. Either tell me, **or** give me the information in written form. (28)
- I feel that since my own children are or have recently been the same age as my students, I am a much better teacher. (5)
- I believe that accepting the individuality of each person is important. There are many "right" answers to questions—some may be better than others—but that doesn't mean a given answer is wrong. (21)
- Leave your problems at home. Present to the students one satisfied or at least well-adjusted adult each class period each day. We may be the only ones they see. (31)
- In dealing with large classes of students, always be alert to the progress of those students who don't particularly stand out for one reason or another. I have students fill out information cards at the beginning of the year so that I can identify some extra-curricular interest in each one. This helps me to realize that each student is a unique human being who has a life outside my classroom. (23)
- I try to operate in my classroom under the touchstone "Don't sweat the small stuff." Calmness and an easy-going atmosphere mean a lot to me in my room. I want students to feel at home with me, but not to the extent of their erasing the distance between themselves and me. I never want a student to feel that he/she can't talk to/with me about things troubling them. Student negative criticism of our col-

leagues sometimes put me at odds with the critics, especially if they put down some teacher I know. I interrupt and insist that "Unless you can say something complimentary, then say nothing at all." But if it continues, I feel badly because, even though these criticisms may be unfounded, they put us all in a bad light. (27)

- I believe that administrators need to hear that they too are doing a good job. They are people just like we are. All of them were "us" once. I view the administrator's role as one of assistance to the building staff. Sometimes administrators may seem to get carried away with an assumed importance, but we all probably make that mistake. It never hurts to remind ourselves that as irreplaceable as we may think we are, the world is filled with other talented professionals who could take our place. (27)
- Parents need to know when students' performance in school is unsatisfactory. We should not rely on administrators to make reports to parents but accept the responsibility ourselves. After all, we teachers are on the front line every hour every day with students. No one knows better than we what's going on in our classrooms. Students sometimes use the classroom as a safe arena to test what they feel may be newly expanding powers. Parents have a right to be kept informed of their son's/daughter's academic **and** social development. (27)
- Expectations of acceptable behavior, excellence in classwork, and treatment of others should be high. Teachers set the tone for success or its absence in the classroom. If we ask for little, we will get little. I believe that we should accept nothing less than what we would want from our own kids. Failure to achieve **all** of our expectations and hopes should not discourage confident teachers who will see every gain as notable. (8)
- I personally feel a teacher's school day doesn't end at 2:45. Some of the most enjoyable and fulfilling time I spend with students is from 2:45-4:00 for Model UN meetings, or on Saturday trips to the Detroit Institute of Art. (19)
- As teachers we should think of ourselves in a certain way as salespeople. We are, in many ways, trying to market knowledge, information and skills. We are trying to convince students and parents of the value of our "product." In this context, we must present ourselves and our product in a manner that will cause our clients to want to "buy" or accept it. (20)

- When parents or administrators request information, I try to respond helpfully. In all matters, mutually supportive and cooperative relationships of respect between parents, teachers, administrators, and students is critically important and need continually to be fostered. I believe that mutual respect enhances a healthy emotional/social/work environment in which students will certainly be the winners. (17)

- One can't take the world's problem on his/her shoulders. Sadly sometimes, one has to close the door to go on with business as usual. (33)

- I've found that when parents know you care, and want their son/daughter to perform as well as is possible, they're appreciative. You've done a little digging to find something good and worthwhile in that student. I know, as a special reading consultant, that the range of ability among low achievers or poorly behaved students is **vast**. Often wrongly, the "gifted" child is perceived as the "well-behaved, good child." We need to find each student's "inside" motivation. Some of our brightest are lazy and irritating to deal with, but when we meet the same person a few years later what a difference! (17)

- I think it is essential for teachers to stay informed of current developments in their teaching field. My teaching field changes constantly, and my curriculum needs to stay current with those changes. Even subtle kinds of changes can be important. During the past few years, I have been able to discuss issues that bother me with students and parents. It is helpful to gather background information in these discussions that provides a better understanding of my students. Often, from my willingness to share a concern with students, I am able to give some useful suggestions. (40)

- I have felt the need to focus on being realistic in terms of time, energy, and commitment to my teaching profession. Especially with a new class in Health Education I have found it important to sort out what seems possible and appropriate, and to be satisfied with my own best efforts. (14)

- In all drafting classes students occasionally have dead-lead time, with either work caught up or not quite enough time to begin the laborious task of making a border and title block on paper. Or maybe it's a "just can't work today" day. I try to have available reasonably current periodicals for these times. Interesting articles can make determined readers of even the slowest readers. (29)

- My students deal with equipment kept in different areas. I test them to make sure they know all locations. (37)
- Communicate with everyone who is anyone in a student's life. Don't give up on anyone. Read *The Prophet;* know what Gibran has to say of the teacher. "If he is indeed wise he does not bid you enter the house of his wisdom, but rather leads you to the threshold of your own mind. . . . " (26)
- Teaching is influenced by our personality, intellect, values, interests. . . .

    Teachers need to be aware of major societal changes and trends. (26)
- By the time most children are ready for kindergarten, the effect of television has made them passive listeners. (26)

    Students want an orderly environment. They'll be supportive. (26)
- Though responsible for it, a person is not his/her conduct. "**What** you did is wrong," not "You're a bad person." (26)
- Utilize student self-interest whenever possible. Use peer pressure to advantage, constructively.

    Consult student records (in Counseling Office) to ascertain students' abilities. Challenge accordingly. Be sure expectations are realistic.

    Strive to treat all students evenly, fairly.
- Some effective teaching practices follow:

    1. Have clear aims: short range daily, hourly lesson plans; long range (semester, year) in line with the prescribed curriculum and school policies.
    2. Be well prepared for each class daily. ("We don't win today's game on yesterday's hits.")
    3. Get attention and interest as soon as possible. Keep students interested mainly by your enthusiasm, preparation, but also by involving them in their own learning process. Ask questions requiring thoughtful responses.
    4. Provide "how to" information. Give specific, concrete examples demonstrating to students the skills they are expected to master — for example: correct usage, vocabulary; logical, criti-

cal thinking; speaking and writing skills; computational skills; appreciation of the national and world history; scientific knowledge and processes; library use; the complexities of art, of the arts, etc.

5. Provide much practice—boardwork, practice sheets, verbal questioning, pop quizzes—to ascertain student understanding and mastery. Verbal and written quizzes help motivate students to study, to learn, and they gain self-confidence as well.

6. When assignments, tests, and quizzes are corrected and recorded, return papers to students. In class, point out common errors. Reteach. Retest.

7. Encourage all students to achieve at the appropriate level. Teacher expectations are usually met if they are realistic and the teacher encourages students. The report card mark is, for some if not most, the strongest but by no means the only means of encouragement.

8. Praise the students, even and especially the least skilled, for effort and accomplishment. Rarely does a student prefer to fail. (35)

- In the course of any given week, teachers may learn students' personal concerns, e.g. "I think I'm pregnant"; "My parents scream and fight all the time—this is destroying our family and I'm very upset"; "My stepfather abuses me sexually; my mother knows, and allows it because she's afraid of him, too."

   When a teenager seeks the counsel of an adult, the matter becomes a sacred trust requiring strict confidentiality. The teacher must tell no one, unless with the student's knowledge, and then only when absolutely necessary to protect or to help the student.

   This personal, private data must **never** be divulged without the utmost care. Certainly, **never** should it be disclosed casually, in any conversation. The Golden Rule applies. Teachers must respect the student's trust with that same respect the teacher expects of another in whom he/she confides. (35)

- Some values and attitudes for education selected and adapted from a list developed by Reo M. Christenson, Professor, Miami (Ohio) University. (*Christian Science Monitor,* January 30, 1987):

1. Acknowledging the importance of self-discipline, defined as the strength to do what we believe we should do, even when we would rather not do it.
2. Being trustworthy and dependable. A person is as good as his/her word.
3. Being honest and truthful, even when it hurts.
4. Having the courage to resist group pressures to do what we would not otherwise choose 'on our own'.
5. Recognizing and respecting the principle of the Common Good; seeking the well-being of the class rather than one's own selfish interests and ends.
6. Practicing good sportsmanship. Recognizing that although the will to win is important, winning is not all-important.
7. Maintaining courtesy in all human relationships.
8. Following the Golden Rule; treating all others as we would wish to be treated.
9. Doing our work well, whatever our work may be. If it is worth doing, it is worth doing well.
10. Showing respect for an appropriate learning environment in the classroom, respect for one's own and other students' right to learn. Respecting classroom and school rules and property.
11. Developing habits that promote physical and emotional health, and refraining from activities destructive of those ends.
12. Recognizing that the most important thing in life is the kind of person we are becoming, the qualities of character and moral behavior we are developing. Students are preparing and being prepared today to be responsible adult citizens of tomorrow. (35)

AFTERWORD

THE IDEA for *Chalk Talks* emerged from my increasing awareness that education in America is at an historic crossroad.

Each year many thousands of excellent teachers retire, taking with them riches of experience and knowledge. The Michigan Public School Employees Retirement System alone approved more than 8,000 retirements for calendar year 1986. (M.E.A. *Voice,* February 2, 1987.) Experts estimate that nationally over one million new teachers will be needed by the 1990s. Many younger teachers now leave the profession, after several years. National concern is real.

In 1986 the Carnegie Forum on Education and the Economy submitted its landmark report: "A Nation Prepared: Teachers for the Twenty-First Century." Presidents Mary Futrell of the National Education Association and Albert Shanker of the American Federation of Teachers were members of the Carnegie Commission which outlined "the need for a national standards board, a major overhaul of teacher education, and **more interaction and professional discussion among teachers in schools.**"

Chalk Talks is one example of this needed "interaction and professional discussion among teachers." Its very existence proves such sharing is possible. Appropriate use of *Chalk Talks* can stimulate and encourage similar interaction and professional discussion in many U.S. schools, and in college education courses as well.

The forty high school teachers and administrators who contributed to *Chalk Talks* — also others who had no time to do so — are dedicated professionals. My own wide teaching experience — in various schools over many years — strongly suggests to me that many high schools have dedicated faculties. I confidently trust that *Chalk Talks* will facilitate similar sharing within such faculties.

As initiator and editor of *Chalk Talks* I envision the possibility of subsequent volumes, new in content. Here I request of you (especially secondary teachers, administrators, and college education professors) a sharing of **your** expertise. Every good teacher has effective techniques; I ask you to share one or several of yours. Selections will appear in future editions of *Chalk Talks,* identified and fully acknowledged as those in this first edition. (I will welcome and appreciate copies of responses to chapter "Questions for Discussion.")

My associates and I offer to serve as forum. You are invited to contribute techniques you use effectively. Reflect, then type, print, or write concrete, specific examples—similar to the selections in *Chalk Talks.*

Send to: CHALK TALKS
Editor and Associates
P.O. Box 6001
Ann Arbor, Michigan 48106

Be sure to include your name, complete address, and phone number. Include also your school name, address, and phone number, as well as the subject and grade you teach.

Your generous contribution of specific techniques will be respected, appreciated, and probably printed in subsequent editions of *Chalk Talks.*

Catherine E. Schwarz

- *Teaching is inseparable from learning. Every good teacher will learn more about his/her subject every year — every month, every week if possible.*

  -Gilbert Highet,
  The Art of Teaching

APPENDIX

- *Report from the classroom, parental note explaining the student's absence: "Please excuse my son's absence from Spanish class. His throat is so sore he can hardly speak English."*

APPENDIX

GIVE HIGH SCHOOL seniors a chance and they will tell you their thoughts about teachers. I did this with twenty-five students in my senior composition class at the end of the year. (June, 1985)

Here are some excerpts from their essays:

Qualities Students Consider Desirable in Teachers

"Teachers who treated us like people were among the most favored. I suppose that personality has most to do with being a 'favored' teacher or just a 'schmuck' teacher."

"Effective teachers have these attributes: discipline, creativity, knowledge and ability to teach, an interest in the subject and in the students, and they are an accessible source of information."

"Good teachers have made a lasting impression on my life. These teachers encouraged me to do my best and never gave up."

"The good teacher has enthusiasm for the subject. **Critical thinking,** not repetition of facts is encouraged."

"Teachers are the most important people . . . the only people besides your parents who help you through life. They do their best to make your life better."

"My favorite teachers really taught me. They brought variety to the classroom by bringing in relevant films, guest speakers, and their own experience."

"A good teacher provides not only classroom discussion but homework and **homethinking** too."

"To reinforce skills taught, he/she takes time in correcting and grading (A, B, C, etc.), returns papers promptly, and requires students to rewrite poor papers."

"Teachers need to research their particular subject area just as a college professor does. Research aids in keeping the teacher's knowledge updated, thereby improving the quality of teaching."

"Teachers I favored had their own opinions and would stick to them. Those teachers were not afraid to debate topics they felt strongly about."

"The good teachers have a type of discipline that isn't harsh or threatening. They make few compromises and carry out discipline for infractions of rules."

"They are patient with their students and try to understand where they're coming from."

"I think the goal of a teacher is to get through to the student. After school a student should be able to remember out of **thinking**, not just memorization."

"As hard as it is for me to say, I think a good teacher should give homework and press students to do it. It's the only way to get the material to stick in."

Importance of Student-Teacher Relationships

"The quality of teacher-student relationships is a key factor in determining a good teacher. He/she is always the teacher and professional first, and then your friend."

"The one who teaches and can carry the title of teacher is one who puts his students first. Students are not there for the teacher. The teacher is there for the student whenever possible."

"They should be there when a student needs a little extra help, and be sure that students know that it is good to ask questions."

"Once a good student-teacher relationship is established, it is easy for students and the teacher to talk. This makes class more interesting because understanding exists."

"The teacher must respect the students and the students must respect the teacher."

"Good teachers talk with the students as people and not **antennae**. It's important to allow people to express ideas and respond to questions in order to give confidence to the students."

"Besides having good relationships with students, good teachers bring in new ideas and current articles which most students enjoy greatly."

Some Students Recognize Their Personal Responsibility

"Gaining knowledge, in the end, is the final decision of the student. He decides whether or not he is willing to make the effort to learn."

"Taking notes may be the biggest bore, but I never regretted taking Algebra notes when, at home, I forgot how to do the problems."

"Practice in class is a very beneficial aspect of learning."

"I've been going to this high school for four years. I've had my run-ins with the good and bad teachers, mostly good. I feel it is also the student's part to make the class good and enjoyable."

Qualities of Poor Teachers

"Throughout one's school years, the teachers are responsible for giving students some of their knowledge. If they have failed at this, they have failed as teachers."

"Poor teachers are bored with their work, do not apply themselves to their job; they just hand out books, dittos, and assignments. No class discussions. Every day is the same, no change of pace to keep class moving and interesting."

"Class is too strict, no flexibility, no fun in learning. Students too worried to ask questions for fear of making the teacher angry."

"Failure to explain expectations clearly."

"Showing favoritism. This discourages others."

"When I went to ask for help, sometimes I received responses like 'I give up. How?' "

"A major factor that set fire to my nerves was when a teacher would never bend a rule. I know rules must proceed, but I was sure that sometimes, when a rule is broken, the teacher did not have to be so stubborn. They should treat us like adults."

"A major problem is lack of communication skills. Nothing is more frustrating than to ask a teacher for help and have them confuse more or throw the problem back at you."

"It is hard to pay attention to someone who lectures continually and doesn't allow you into the discussion to express your ideas."

"Poor teachers don't want to be yelled at and are afraid of criticism, so they let the class run out of control."

"If they don't teach at all, but just assign work and give tests, they should be called 'correctors,' not teachers."

"Bad teachers? Those are the ones I try to forget. Some are 'bad' not because they're not knowledgeable, or because they don't care, but because they don't know how to teach."

"Some people just don't belong in the teaching profession. They are the ones who pass out dittos, don't correct your work and make you watch endless movies. These are the ones most of us would like to forget, but unfortunately they make 'lasting impressions' also. This is certainly not fair because we are cheated out of a chance to learn and to gain."

"Of bad teachers I've had, most were apathetic toward the students. One sure way to wind up on the bad list is to favor a few students and leave the others to the side."

"Teachers who waste much valuable class time tending to personal needs, like balancing a checkbook, tend to turn the class off. These few give teachers a bad name."

"Something I believe hurts the students is to turn in their assignments and then find out that the teacher doesn't even read them."

"Some teachers don't seem to care about the students' feelings nor have compassion for those having difficulty in the class."

"The poor teacher is not organized or prepared for class. Having assigned work of little importance, he/she takes little time to review the work of students and grades with a simple check (✔). His tests are inadequate because they have been used for years and consequently circulated around the school."

"It's not always the teacher's fault. Some students just don't want to learn. Also, sometimes the teacher is forced into a subject he does not enjoy teaching. Teachers shouldn't be taken advantage of either."

"The classroom atmosphere of a poor teacher is usually chaotic because the teacher is not organized. The absence of applied rules also promotes a lack of respect for the teacher."

"I have experienced both 'good' and 'poor' teachers. One type has enriched my life and taught me so that I may continue my education. The other type of teacher has disappointed me and cheated me of some precious time and knowledge. However, neither type of teacher is completely responsible for the enrichment or deprivation of my education. The student has a responsibility to himself, because to a certain extent you get out of education what you put into it."

Concluding Comments of Students

"As you begin to mature and develop, you begin to understand the value of education in your life. That is also when you begin to value your teachers and not take what they have to offer for granted."

"It's important to allow people to express ideas and respond to questions in order to give confidence to students."

"The good teachers don't possess all the good qualities—just quite a few of them. The good teachers are the ones students remember and are the people to whom they give their wholehearted thanks for a well-rounded education."

* * * * *

Schools exist primarily for the education of the young. The best schools and best teachers elicit the cooperation and active participation of students in their own intellectual growth. Good teachers know that listening to students—their thoughts and views, as well as their satisfactions, dissatisfactions and recommendations—is wise, even crucial. (35)

CONTRIBUTORS

1. Bologna, Richard
   Principal

2. Brucker, James
   Special Education

3. Crane, William
   Counseling and Guidance

4. Daily, Jean
   Special Education

5. Davio, Barbara
   Business and Data Processing

6. DeBurton, Eileen
   Foreign Language

7. DeMars, Geraldine
   Business

8. Edgeworth, Michael
   Science

9. Florida, Waymon
   English

10. Galbraith, Sandra S.
    English

11. Grecu, Mary Lee
    Social Studies and Business

12. Hancotte, Phyllis
    Special Education

13. Hyatt, Janice
    English

14. Ivkovich, Virginia
   Health Occupations and Vocational
15. Johnson, Linda
   English
16. Kelly, Michael
   Social Studies
17. Krause, Kenneth
   English and Reading
18. Lawing, Sylvia
   English
19. Loesche, Steven
   Social Studies
20. Manor, Steven
   Social Studies
21. Marshall, Leann
   Vocational and Business
22. Mezga, Betty J.
   Social Studies
23. Millar, Duane
   Foreign Language
24. Musolf, Beverly
   Mathematics
25. Noud, Laurient
   Industrial Arts
26. Okey, Ted N.
   Assistant Principal
27. Parrish, Douglas
   Foreign Language
28. Peterson, Richard M.
   Industrial Arts
29. Powelson, Bruce
   Industrial Arts
30. Recker, Bonnie
   English

31. Rein, Marlene
    English
32. Rice, Susan
    Library and Media
33. Saoud, Joanne
    English and Drama
34. Schafer, Randy
    Industrial Arts
35. Schwarz, Catherine
    English
36. Skinner, Betty C.
    Business
37. Stepp, Geneva
    Home Economics
38. Sweet, Nancy
    Mathematics
39. Turner, James
    Social Studies
40. Woodruff, Marilyn
    Home Economics

(Contributions are identified by the number in parenthesis after each statement.)

Departments represented in *Chalk Talks:*

Administration	Library and Media
Business	Mathematics
Counseling and Guidance	Science
Data Processing	Social Studies
English	Special Education
Foreign Language	Technical and Industrial
Health Occupations	Vocational Education
Home Economics	

■

ABOUT THE EDITOR

Catherine E. Schwarz holds an M.A. in History (University of Detroit), an M.A. in Counseling (University of Michigan), and additional graduate credits from Purdue University, Arizona State University, Eastern Michigan University.

She has been a member of the Howell High School faculty since January, 1969, principally in the English department—but including three years in the Counseling Office. Before coming to Howell she taught many years in private schools at elementary and secondary levels. She has had experience as well in university and community college teaching, and in private practice as a career counselor. She lives with her husband in Ann Arbor, Michigan.

A. M. D. G.